THE 50 TOUGHEST QUESTIONS
MY CLERGY & COUNSELLING FRIENDS ARE
REGULARLY ASKED

QUESTIONS
&
RESPONSES

ROWLAND CROUCHER

COVENTRY
PRESS

Published in Australia by
Coventry Press
33 Scoresby Road
Bayswater Vic. 3153
Australia

ISBN 9780648323310

Copyright © Rowland Croucher 2018

All rights reserved. Other than for the purposes and subject to the conditions prescribed under the *Copyright Act*, no part of this publication may be reproduced, stored in a retrieval system, or transmitted in any form or by any means, electronic, mechanical, photocopying, recording or otherwise, without the prior permission of the publisher.

Unless otherwise indicated, Scripture quotations are from the *New Revised Standard Version Bible*, copyright 1989, Division of Christian Education of the National Council of the Churches of Christ in the United States of America. Used by permission. All rights reserved.

Cataloguing-in-Publication entry is available from the National Library of Australia http:/catalogue.nla.gov.au/.

Text design by Filmshot Graphics (FSG)
Cover design by Ian James – www.jgd.com.au

Printed in Australia

Contents

Introduction 4

Chapter 1 9
Abuse: 'Pastor, I'm in trouble.'

Chapter 2 25
Mavericks: what shall we do with today's prophets?

Chapter 3 36
TED Talk: Let's make it simple - what would Jesus do?

Chapter 4 44
Jesus' 'key to understanding': love

Chapter 5 53
Social justice (1)
How to know the Lord – what is social justice?

Chapter 6 59
Social justice [2]
Doing justice - so where do we begin?

Chapter 7 68
Dom Helder Camara: a modern saint who seriously followed Jesus

Chapter 8 77
Pharisees ancient and modern

Chapter 9 84
Why most do - but some don't – believe in the existence of God

Chapter 10 99
Billy Graham
Life, ministry and legacy

Chapter 11 108
Is Gandhi in heaven?
Christianity and other religions

Epilogue 118
Dealing with grief

Postscript 128
Coming up in future volumes

INTRODUCTION

A few years ago, I was asked how long I'd spent in a 50-year pastoral counselling career listening to people with problems. A quick calculation led to the astonishing figure of about 25,000 hours. That did not include socialising.

This little book - hopefully a series of books - seeks to address what I believe are the most common/complex/urgent of the issues people raise with me.

An important note: our title is 'Questions and Responses' not 'Questions and Answers'. There's a reason for that. Individuals can posit 'answers' to many questions that they might have figured out for themselves; but others have travelled a different route that led to different 'answers'.

Only God (presuming God exists - we'll get to that) has answers to everything. I've never met or heard of a human being who can legitimately make the same claim.

IT'S OK TO ASK QUESTIONS - AND PERHAPS EVEN CHANGE YOUR MIND!

I was brought up in a small Plymouth Brethren 'assembly' (they believed only apostate Christian groups used the word 'church'). It was actually a benign sect: they had it all figured out. I cannot recall my late father changing his mind on anything substantial. But his eldest son (*moi*) had a severe disability: I was constantly asking questions. My father's handicap: he was allergic to questions. 'Rowland, don't ask so many questions: just believe!' he would intone.

I took part of his advice to heart: I stopped asking *him* questions. But I have refused all my life to believe something simply because an authority-figure tells me to...

As a teenager, I wrote a series of questions and sent them to our elders. 'Noah's flood: where did enough water come from to cover Mt Everest? How did Noah get Australian koalas to the Middle East and deliver them Downunder again? And how did sloths - which can't swim - get back to Latin America? And if we're the only group - of the world's 30-40,000 Christian denominations - to get all our 'doctrines' right, what do we make of people like the great missionary Hudson Taylor?' Etc. etc. A scholarly elder, Mr Tom Carson, responded: 'Ah, Rowland, just imagine how much more effective he would have been if he'd belonged with us...'

Those elders 'just believed.' I heard one of them say, 'If the Bible said Jonah swallowed the whale, yes, I'd believe that.'

Subsequently, after a few careers encouraging people to ask questions - as a high school teacher, pastor, and wandering prophet on Australia's tertiary campuses - I spent three years doing a Masters' degree at the University of Sydney in Social Psychology, exploring 'The Diffusion of Innovations in Religious Organisations' (how religious groups change).

What did I learn? In summary:

* The ideological spectrum is shaped like a bell-curve: with 'early adopters' (these days 'innovators') at one end and 'laggards' (today 'maintainers') at the other. Or, from left to right, radicals-progressives-conservatives-fundamentalists...

* Most people's belief-systems develop from someone (perhaps an opinion-leader with some perceived credibility) getting hold of them when they were impressionable...

* The 'reinforcement effect' is strongest if one belongs to a group of people with similar beliefs...

And so on...

A case can be made that all prophets/leaders in the Hebrew/Christian tradition radically changed their minds: it's called *metanoia*, 'repentance'. Two classic stories: Saul of Tarsus (Acts 9), and Jesus' close friend Peter (Acts 10).

And Jesus' church has subsequently experienced several 'paradigm shifts' throughout its history (google Thomas Kuhn then Hans Kung on all that). The latest, which is overtaking us with 'whitewater speed' as America's premier public theologian Dr Martin Marty puts it, is the genuine acceptance of LGBTIQs in more of our minds/churches.

This should not surprise us. We've been there before - relatively recently - on many other similarly broad issues: like slavery/racism, acceptance of Jews (remember Luther's encouragement to 'burn [these Christ-killers'] houses and synagogues'?), women in leadership, accepting divorcees, etc.

How do we handle these attacks on our long-held prejudices? Four ways, according to the hermeneutic commonly labelled as 'the Wesleyan Quadrilateral': Scripture, informed by Reason, Tradition and Experience.

All very nice, but still inadequate. What changed the Apostle Paul's mind? The serenity, courage and faith of Stephen, and others he'd persecuted? Yes. The voice he'd heard on the Damascus road? Maybe. But I reckon the 'clincher' was the greeting by a Christ-follower, Ananias: 'Brother Saul'.

Without love and acceptance, all our fancy creedal rhetoric is, as Paul later wrote, like a 'noisy gong or a clanging symbol'...

ooOoo

In another life - in the 1970s - I was the Victorian media spokesperson for the conservative *Festival of Light* (it's something like America's *Focus on the Family*). One night, Peter Couchman, a genial ABC TV interviewer, asked me to join him and two women from the *Prostitutes' Collective* to discuss some issues on live TV. In the middle of it all, one of the women turned to me and asked, 'Why do you Christians hate us?' I mumbled a response saying I didn't think I hated anyone...

But as I drove home that night, her question troubled me and has done so ever since. Why do we Christians - especially of the Conservative Evangelical and/or Fundamentalist variety - come across so often as moralistic bigots? We're more like Pharisees (for whom 'repentance precedes acceptance'), than our Master, Jesus ('acceptance preceding and encouraging repentance').

That woman's question has helped me change my mind on a few things.

And I resigned from the *Festival of Light*.

ooOoo

When someone makes an appointment to see me, a 'generalist' pastoral counsellor, what do we talk about? Short answer: anything at all that's important for them.

I generally walk with counselees (if the Melbourne weather is friendly), and most - not all - counselling sessions fit into the classic 'fifty minute hour'. We agree to 'jump into the deep end' and I give an assurance that I will respect my friend's confidentiality. Within the first five minutes - after some 'small talk' - I invite my parishioner/client to 'give me a headline or two'.

Some of the questions are memorable (I've altered a few details here and there):

- 'Rowland, I used to belong to a [criminal] gang. Recently, I've been going to church and I heard about the need to "confess your sins to one another". Well, I killed [several] people during those wild years... And nobody else knows... '
- Undergrad student: 'We're doing philosophy, and recently studied the so-called "proofs" for God's existence. My evangelical friend says he's impressed by the "first cause" idea. I reckon there could have been an infinite regression of causes...'
- 'Pastor, I'm in my fifties now, and I've never had a close relationship with a man. I'd love to have been a mother, but it's too late. I have a strong sexual drive and my way of dealing with that is to pleasure myself. My pastor, however, is a fundamentalist who reckons people go to hell for doing that. I'm scared and often sleepless about it all. What do you think?'
- [To a troubled teenager]: 'What do you want to do with your life, Angela?' 'Oh, kill a couple of people who seriously abused me... and burn down the government welfare agency that was supposed to care for me'

Chapter 1
ABUSE: 'Pastor, I'm in trouble.'

ABUSE, VIOLENCE, WAR

> *She came to talk to me in our church office after being discharged from hospital, and still wore the bruises her violent husband had inflicted on her. 'I'm not taking this abuse any more', she said. 'You don't have to', I responded, knowing something of the ongoing saga. I phoned a friend with a large property and a few spare rooms, and before the day was out she had transferred herself and her two children to that safe haven. The enraged husband contacted me and told me he'd be coming after me with a gun...*

In this chapter, abuse refers to any action between human beings which intentionally harms or injures another. The context can include physical, emotional, institutional (including legal/ military), spiritual or sexual violence - or a combination of these...

This chapter has half the story: the bad/violent half. See chapters 4-6 on Love and Justice for the responses I believe Jesus might make/encourage. [1]

BUT FIRST, FEEL/THINK ABOUT THESE...

- Regarding abuse in some religious settings: Emile Durkheim said religion serves to strengthen the bonds of solidarity among those who worship the same god in the same way. But the flip side of this solidarity is enmity towards those who worship other gods or worship the same god differently.

- Martin Luther King: 'There may have been a time when war served as a negative good by preventing the spread and growth of an evil force, but the very destructive power of modern weapons of warfare eliminates even the possibility that war may any longer serve as a negative good. And so, if we assume that life is worth living, if we assume that mankind has a right to survive, then we must find an alternative to war.' [2] [3]

Here's a potpourri of terrible stories to give us an idea of the magnitude of evil in our sad world..

* 'Yazidis in the Middle East have undergone centuries of persecution - including, according to one estimate, 72 genocides. Awful stories of atrocities committed against them are coming to light: ISIS moving people without providing food and water; the prisoners were so desperate they had to drink from the latrines. From an ISIS manual on 'Questions and Answers on Taking Captives and Slaves' one question asked: Is it permissible to have intercourse with a female slave who has not yet reached puberty? The answer was yes. [4]

* The genocide of 1.5 million Armenians carried out during and after World War I was implemented in two phases: the wholesale killing of the able-bodied male population through massacre and subjection of army conscripts to forced labour; followed by the deportation of women, children, the elderly, and the infirm on death marches leading to the Syrian desert. Driven forward by military escorts, the deportees were deprived of food and water and subjected to periodic robbery, rape, and massacre. [5]

* Asia Bibi, a Pakistani Christian mother of five, was sentenced to death under the nation's blasphemy law for drinking from the same water as Muslims. She has been held on death row in Pakistan for more than seven years. [6]

* The election of Rodrigo Duterte in the Philippines has resulted in 1000 people a month being killed as a result of his 'war on drugs'. One newspaper headline: 'So many die in the war on drugs that even the funeral directors are complaining.'

* Then there's the seemingly endless war in Syria. 'I'm just a headline: the bad President, the bad guy who is killing all the good guys' (Bashar Assad, President of Syria, referring to the nearly half a million citizens killed during the first five and a half years of his nation's civil war, including those who died from alleged war crimes perpetrated by his administration). Assad blamed a 'narrative' propagated by the U.S. government. But how do we explain the photographs (of 28,000 tortured bodies) carried by 'Caesar' who fled Syria in August 2013? [7]

* Also 'The Troubles' (1968-1998) - a violent thirty-year conflict framed by a civil rights march in Londonderry on 5 October 1968 and the Good Friday Agreement on 10 April 1998. At the heart of the conflict lay the constitutional status of Northern Ireland. The goal of the unionist and overwhelmingly Protestant majority was to remain part of the United Kingdom. The goal of the nationalist and republican, almost exclusively Catholic, minority was to become part of the Republic of Ireland. [8]

* World-wide, Muslims kill more people than anyone else, don't they? Well, maybe, but Americans kill more Americans than Muslims do; British kill British; Indonesians kill Indonesians; Chinese kill Chinese. A Westerner's chance of being slain by a terrorist is very small: perhaps our fear is increased by spectacular events like 9/11 or the Paris episodes, and, more recently, trucks and cars being driven into crowds of pedestrians...

* And let us feel appropriate shame at the general inability/willingness of Western nations (including my own, Australia) to stop persecutions of ethnic groups all over the world... Why do militant Buddhists in Myanmar get away with abusing the Rohingya people? Item: 'Eyewitnesses have reported shocking cases, including soldiers dragging a woman in labour from her house, and beating her in the stomach with a stick, then stomping the baby to death under their boots. In another awful instance, a 25-year-old woman was gang-raped by five soldiers. Her eight-month-old son was killed with a knife after crying out.' [9]

* Remember when American B-52 bombers dropped more than 500,000 tons of explosives on Cambodia's countryside? During just 200 nights in 1973, 257,456 tons of explosives fell in secret carpet-bombing sweeps. The pilots flew at such heights that they were incapable of discriminating between a village and their targets, North Vietnamese supply lines. The bombs were so massive they blew out the eardrums of anyone standing within a kilometre radius. According to one genocide researcher, up to 500,000 Cambodians were killed, many of them children. [10]

SEXUAL ABUSE

> *I'm thinking now of three abused women - three of many hundreds I've counselled over the years. They were raped repeatedly by their biological fathers: two of them until their teenage years. And each of these now middle-aged women also had emotionally cold/distant mothers: at least two of those mothers certainly knew what was happening when 'daddy' was 'cuddling' their little baby/girl...*

Abuse victims have their own preferred approach to talking about their deep pain. These three 'survivors' had hazy memories of when it all began. One of them wanted to re-live the terrible episodes in detail. Another shared her deep painful feelings about it all. A third talked about the awful events or conversations throughout her adult life that 'triggered' terrible and traumatic memories…

Every 'people-helper', psychologist, or counselling pastor hears many stories of serious abuse suffered by children at the hands of the Big People in their young lives...

A significant book was recently published in Australia - *Crimes of the Father* - by one of our greatest contemporary writers, Tom Keneally. Christian religious institutions have had a poor track record of supporting people who were sexually abused. They have tax-exempt status and seem to be more concerned about their finances or reputation…

In many parts of the world, the horrors of what happened in these institutions which were supposed to care for children have come under the scrutiny of Royal Commissions and other investigative bodies. These enquiries were prompted often by adult survivors 'coming out' with their horrific stories.

Sometimes news media prompted the enquiry (the role of the Boston *Globe's* investigative team and the award-winning movie *Spotlight* come to mind).

In a submission to Australia's *Royal Commission into Institutional Responses to Child Sexual Abuse,* Vatican advisor Baroness Sheila Hollins wrote that clergy may have used canon law to hide alleged sexual offending in their ranks. 'Canon law may have been deliberately misused to excuse inexcusable behaviour, and to cover up known wrongdoing', the member of the Pontifical Commission for the Protection of Minors wrote. Canon lawyer and whistle-blower priest Father Thomas Doyle told the hearing that the Australian Catholic church authorities have been aware of allegations of clerical child sexual abuse for decades. 'Canon law has been used as an excuse in some instances by ecclesiastical authorities for not proceeding and taking direct action against reports of child sexual abuse', he said. The commission heard that 'pontifical secrecy' - the church's highest form of secrecy outside the confessional - was still in force in relation to child sexual abuse. 'If there are no civil laws requiring reporting, then the pontifical secret still applies.' [11]

> *A boy in an elite Australian school was sexually abused by its Boarding School master. The school failed to conduct any investigation, but instead, the boy was expelled. In the Royal Commission investigating such complaints, the excuse is commonly proffered: 'They acted as best they could in difficult circumstances according to the knowledge and practices of the times'.*

My response? 'Rubbish!'

Then there was the inadequate police response to the exposure of an online site posting thousands of explicit images of underage girls without their knowledge or consent. Queensland Police concluded that the site did not 'appear to contain any child exploitation material', and one young woman told Radio Triple J's *Hack* program that she had received exceptionally short shrift from police when she made a complaint about her image being on the site: 'The guy I spoke to, an older guy, just laughed. He said that's what I get for taking them'. An example of deeply entrenched victim-blaming attitudes in Australia.

ABUSE OF MINORITIES

Isis zealots throw gay men from tall buildings. But it's happened in Australia (simply substitute 'cliffs' for 'tall buildings'). On a December day in 1988, a teenager on a spearfishing expedition found a body at the bottom of one of the wild, honey-coloured sandstone cliffs that line Sydney Harbour. Scott Johnson, a gay man, had moved to Australia to be with his partner and was pursuing his doctorate at the Australian National University in Canberra. He was a 'virtuoso' mathematician. The day he disappeared, Scott Johnson told his Ph.D. supervisor, Ross Street of Sydney's Macquarie University, that he'd had a breakthrough on a vexing problem that was crucial to his dissertation... [12]

About eighty men died or disappeared across NSW from the late 70s to early 90s during an epidemic of gay hate crimes. Many of the brutal attacks on these men happened in the eastern suburbs which was a hunting ground for gangs of young thugs such as the Bondi Boys and the Tamarama Three: it was not difficult to make these murders look like suicides. [13]

Speaking of police and minorities, Terrence Cunningham, president of the International Association of Chiefs of Police, apologised for what he called 'the role that our profession has played in society's historical mistreatment of communities of colour' at the group's convention on 17 October 2016. [14]

Which leads us to the Australian frontier wars - a series of conflicts fought between Indigenous Australians and mainly British settlers that spanned a total of 146 years. The first fighting took place several months after the landing of the First Fleet in January 1788 and the last clashes occurred as late as 1934. Historian Henry Reynolds has suggested a figure of about 30,000 indigenous people killed since white settlement - a figure now tacitly accepted by more conservative scholars like historian Professor Geoffrey Blainey. The most common estimates of European fatalities range from 2,000 to 2,500. [15]

There were many killings, a famous one being the 1838 Myall Creek massacre in which 28 people were slaughtered at Myall Creek near Inverell, NSW. On the shore near Portland in Victoria was one of the largest recorded massacres when whalers and the local Kilcarer clan of the Gunditjmara people disputed rights to a beached whale carcass. Reports vary but 60 to 200 Aborigines died, including women and children. [16]

In Australia, we have a right-wing 'black armband theory' about dealing with the collective guilt of all this. Here's a graphic excerpt from Jan Roberts, *Massacres to Mining: the Colonisation of Aboriginal Australia:* 'The following story is recalled by Aborigines today. It comes from the high country in northeast Victoria. Old Mr. Birt would tell it. He had heard it from his mother who was of the Ya-idthma-dthang Tribe:

> *"My mother would sit and cry and tell me this: they buried our babies in the ground with only their heads above the ground. All in a row they were. Then they had a test to see who could kick the babies' heads off the furthest. One man clubbed a baby's head off from horse-back. Then they spent most of the day raping the women, most of them were then tortured to death by sticking sharp things like spears up their vaginas until they died..." [17] [18]*

How do the biblical prophets deal with all this? One example: Jesus' follower Stephen to the Jewish authorities [Acts 7:51]: 'You stiff-necked people, uncircumcised in heart and ears, you always resist the Holy Spirit. As your ancestors did, so do you.' This prophetic idea of identification with oppressors is contrary to the 'I wasn't there, don't blame me' response.

Walter Brueggemann's *The Prophetic Imagination* (2nd edition, Augsburg Fortress, 2001) is a classic on these sorts of questions: 'Jesus in his solidarity with the marginal ones is moved to compassion. Compassion constitutes a radical form of criticism, for it announces that the hurt is to be taken seriously, that the hurt is not to be accepted as normal and natural, but is an abnormal and unacceptable condition for humanness...'

The closest an Australian leader has got to acknowledging our role in all this, and identifying with past evil oppressors, is probably ex-Prime Minister Paul Keating's Redfern speech, which brilliantly attacked the 'We weren't there; you can't blame us!' black armband denial of responsibility for our ancestors' evil oppressions...

FAMILY VIOLENCE

... is an epidemic in our world.

> **Fact Check:** *Violence by a partner or former partner is the leading preventable cause of death and illness of women aged 15 to 45 in Australia. More than one woman a week is being slain in this way... One in four Australian women has experienced at least one incident of violence from an intimate partner (2,194,200, 25.1 per cent) since the age of 15. [19]*

An Australian Institute of Criminology paper said that 'in the vast majority of cases, children's abusers are known to them'. According to the Australian Institute of Family Studies the prevalence of child sexual abuse is 1.4-8 per cent for penetrative abuse and 5.7-16 per cent for non-penetrative abuse for boys and 4-12 per cent for penetrative abuse and 13.9-36 per cent for non-penetrative abuse for girls... To put those figures into context, the 'best case' scenario is that 1 in 20 boys is sexually abused. The worst case is that one in three girls is. Yes, women can also abuse, but as the AIFS 'Who Abuses Children?' fact sheet makes clear, 'Evidence overwhelmingly indicates that the majority of child sexual abuse is perpetrated by males'.

What can parents do to prevent/restrict these possibilities of abuse? Here's one radical approach:

> *'When our first daughter was born, my husband and I made a family rule: no man would ever babysit our children. No exceptions. This includes male relatives and friends and even extracurricular and holiday programs, such as basketball camp, where men can have unrestricted and unsupervised access to children... Group slumber parties are also out. When there is a group of excited children it is far too easy for one of them to be lured away by a father or older brother without being noticed. To be clear, I'm not saying that all men are sexual predators.' [20]*

SO WHAT CAN I DO?

Let's start with Bonhoeffer's famous quote: 'Not to speak is to speak. Not to act is to act'. Or the American civil rights leader Congressman John Lewis: 'If not us, then who? If not now, then when?' Walking away/being silent when someone's being harassed or bullied can be an act of cowardice - or, naturally, of self-preservation. Our rationales may include these: 'It's none of my business.' 'I'll get hurt.' 'I don't have the power to stop the bullying.' 'There's nothing I can do...' And so on.

Research has found that there are bystanders in 87% of bullying situations. Unfortunately, our cowardice or selfishness leads us to be ostrich-like, when we could be influential in exercising more power than we realise we have. Parents and teachers have a strategic role in encouraging children to become helpful bystanders and by letting them know that adults will support them, if and when they report a misdemeanour. We also have a role in highlighting the courage of those who paid a high price - even with their lives - for resisting evil...

There are also reasons why people who take the New Testament and the teaching of Jesus seriously are frequently pacifists. It is a significant challenge for any preacher to use the New Testament in clear support of war, even a just war. For, at some level, all violence is a betrayal of Christian commitment - as Jesus makes clear in dismissing the 'punitive psychology' of his own disciples in Luke's Gospel when they, in the face of rejection, seek vengeful recompense in the form of 'fire from heaven' (Luke 9:54).

'What would Jesus do?' I have a habit of asking Christians 'What did Jesus say to the adulterous woman?' (John 8:1-11). If they're conservative, they'll mostly respond 'Go and sin no more', forgetting that Jesus first said 'I do not condemn you!' In his short essay 'Writings in the Dust', former Anglican Archbishop of Canterbury Rowan Williams posits that when Jesus paused to sketch in the dirt in front of the adulterous woman and the people who wanted to stone her, he is creating an opportunity for alternatives beyond stoning her. He is opening a space for everyone to consider their situation, to breathe.

BACK TO WAR AND PEACE

> *Raoul Wallenberg, a Swedish diplomat, was credited with helping thousands of Hungarian Jews flee Nazi-controlled Germany during the Holocaust. But he mysteriously vanished in 1945. Authorities pronounced him dead on October 26, 2016, after receiving a request from his family to do so. (But newly published diaries of a KGB officer tell us Wallenberg was liquidated on Stalin's orders in 1947.)*

And before we cast a stone at anyone else, we Christians will pause to remember our bloody past. To quote just one terrible episode (in the words of America's premier public theologian Martin Marty): 'Those with historical senses could recall what Catholic-Lutheran actions used to be like. For instance, through the first centuries after the start of the Protestant Reformation, [celebrated] in 2017 after 500 years… Catholics and Lutherans by the thousands killed each other. They got mixed up on both sides of a Thirty Years' War, whose Christian devastation provides cheerless comparison to Muslim-related conflicts in Syria and elsewhere today.' [21]

CONCLUSION

For my sober reflection, I sometimes visit Wikipedia's 'Lists of Wars by Death Toll'. Excerpt:

> *World War 2 (1939-1945) - 40-85 million; Mongol Conquests (1206-1324) - 40-70 million; Taiping Rebellion (1850-1864) - 20-100 million; Three Kingdoms War (184-280) - 36-40 million; Conquest of the Americas (1492-1691)*

- 8,400,000 - 137,750,000; Chinese Civil War (1927-1949) - 8 million; Russian Civil War and Foreign Intervention (1917-1922) - 5-9 million; Thirty Years' War (1618-1648) - 3-11.5 million (the German mortality rate was 15-20% due to a mix of armed conflict, famine and disease); Napoleonic Wars (1803-1815) - 3.5 - 6 million. And then, the French Wars of Religion (1562-1598) - 2-4 million

ooOoo

Finally, be challenged by this...

I remember the things we do and don't do to each other:
war, injustice,
poverty, torture,
broken relationships, bullying, meanness, gossip,
betrayal,
I remember,
but sometimes I'd rather forget
Yeah, I'd rather forget
Denial tempts me
Because I don't care?
or because I care too much?
or because I want to do something about it,
or because I don't know what to do
I don't know what to do.
Maybe I'll try a different verb
Maybe I'll feel for a time
Can I let my spirit take in the weight of the pain
without bouncing into a flurry of fixing? [22]

Footnotes

[1] There's also more bad news in the RACISM chapter (in a future volume in this series, including some observations on current and previous slave trades...)

[2] On Christmas Eve, 1967, the Canadian Broadcasting Corporation aired this sermon as part of the seventh annual Massey Lectures.

[3] More... see the brilliant summary of 'Just War Theories' here: http://www.iep.utm.edu/justwar/

[4] *Weekend Australian Magazine*, 12-13 November 2016, pp. 29 ff.

[5] For a well-researched article, plus pictures, visit https://en.wikipedia.org/wiki/Armenian_Genocide

[6] *The Melbourne Anglican,* November 2016, p. 5.

[7] *The Australian*, 8 February 2017, p. 9. On the other hand, let us not forget the endless American drone strikes in the region...

[8] http://www.bbc.co.uk/history/troubles . This was mainly a territorial conflict, rather than a religious one. At its heart lay two mutually exclusive visions of national identity and national belonging. Over 3600 people were killed and thousands more injured...

[9] *The Age* editorial, 16 March 2017. The world was surprised when Time in 2013 ran a cover-story featuring 'The Face of Buddhist Terror' - about a monk named Wirathu whose ultra-nationalist *Ma Ba Tha* movement advocates race and religious laws against Muslims.

[10] A headline in the world's press this week - March 12, 2017 - says Washington wants Cambodia to repay a $500 million 'war debt', a demand which has prompted indignation and outrage in Phnom Penh.

[11] *The Age*, 10 February 2017, p. 8. One of Australia's worst sexual abusers was Father Gerald Ridsdale, who was convicted of nearly 140 offences with more than 50 confirmed victims in ten Victorian Catholic parishes. His bishop tore up church records to conceal his offending...

[12] https://www.nytimes.com/2017/01/30/world/australia/australia-gay-men-killed-suicides-sydney.html.

[13] Google Duncan McNab, whose book on the subject is titled *Getting Away with Murder*. There have been quite a few press articles on all this: and the consensus is that the police were slow to investigate many of the crimes...

[14] *Time*, 31 October 2016, p. 4.

[15] https://en.wikipedia.org/wiki/Australian_frontier_wars

[16] See the (incomplete) list of massacre here: https://en.wikipedia.org/wiki/List_of_massacres_of_Indigenous_Australians

[17] Jan Roberts, *Massacres to Mining: the Colonisation of Aboriginal Australia*, 1981/1985, p. 19.

[18] Also visit this long list of websites: http://treatyrepublic.net/content/britain-worlds-worst-mass-murderer. Note also that many of Australia's Aboriginal people have died since 1789 from diseases like smallpox against which they had no resistance.

[19] Australia's National Research Organisation for Women's Safety (ANROWS). The "One in Three" campaign is a group of diverse advocates who raise awareness of male victims of domestic violence; they say that one in three victims of family violence is male.

[20] Kasey Edwards, *Guilt Trip: My Quest To Leave The Baggage Behind*, Black Inc., 2017.
[21] Martin Marty, 'Sightings', 22 August 2016.
[22] Excerpt from a poetic sermon by Michele Rizoli, Toronto United Mennonite Church November 2010. Scripture Text: Matthew 5, Micah 6:8

Chapter 2
MAVERICKS: what shall we do with today's prophets?

In this chapter, we'll look at one of three ways people handle many significant ideas/life choices: the mavericks. (The others, for future chapters: the honest doubters, and the person who has 'faith'. Part of my thesis: these three attitudes are not necessarily mutually exclusive).

Henry Ford once hired an efficiency expert to evaluate his company. After a few weeks, he reported favourably except for one thing: 'It's that man down the hall. Every time I go to his office, he's just sitting there with his feet on his desk. He's wasting your money'.

'That man', replied Mr Ford, 'once had an idea that saved us millions of dollars. At the time I believe his feet were planted right where they are now'.

An IBM commercial put it this way: 'We have forty-six people like that, and we don't worry about where they put their feet either. Their job is to generate ideas, but under a very special condition. It's called freedom. Freedom from deadlines. Freedom from committees. Freedom from the usual limits of corporate approval. We may not always understand what they are doing, much less how they do it. But we know this: the best way to inspire such people is to get out of the way'.

Samuel Maverick (1803-1870) was a Texan rancher who for some reason didn't put a brand on some of his calves. So an unbranded animal on the open range came to be called a 'maverick' and anyone who found such an animal could put their own brand on them...

So a maverick, according to my online dictionaries, is 1: an unbranded range animal; especially: a motherless calf; 2: an independent individual who does not go along with a group or party. They refuse to play by the rules. They're not scared to cross the line of conformity; but their unorthodox tactics get results! [1]

Mavericks refuse to be confined by conventional beliefs or mores. The Protestant 'Dissenters' or Nonconformists refused to believe that simply because a church was 'Established' it was therefore The Only True Church. M. Scott Peck says the most common response by readers of his first best-seller, *The Road Less Travelled*, was that he'd written nothing new 'but rather that I've written the kinds of things readers have been thinking all along but were afraid to talk about. "What a relief it was to know I wasn't wrong," they've told me, "to know I wasn't crazy".' [2]

Somewhere in his book *In Search of Stones* (Simon & Schuster, 1995), Peck ('an ex-WASP') says he enjoys ordering just two entrees and a dessert and watching the response on the face of the waiter. I do that sometimes. (So now I know I'm not crazy.)

The Hebrew-Christian tradition is full of mavericks. There's Noah, the only person who with his family believed God was serious about punishing evil with a flood. And Abraham, unique among the inhabitants of Canaan to believe in one God rather than many fertility gods. And Job, who didn't go along with the common notion that suffering is always a punishment for wrongdoing. And Paul, the only ex-Pharisee to be an author of various books of Holy Scripture.

The best mavericks are both gifted and passionate. Noam Chomsky is an example of what can be achieved when intellectual brilliance is married to a radical stance. The Western press is not really 'free', he tells us. Gore Vidal is another, and John Pilger. The list goes on.

One of Australia's best-known mavericks is Philip Adams. I disagree with him on just about every religious opinion he holds. But I like him. I like Scott Peck too, in spite of some unorthodox religious ideas in his books (and his notion in The Road Less Travelled that adultery may sometimes be therapeutic - an opinion he later recanted). Manning Clark is another Australian maverick. (Every conservative Christian should read - in his two-volumed autobiography - his scathing denunciation of 'religious frowners').

Mavericks, nonconformists, dissenters are 'different'. They conceptualise ideas in terms of 'paradigm shifts' (a term coined by Thomas Kuhn in his book *The Structure of Scientific Revolutions* in 1961) - an attempt to describe the changes that occur in Belief Systems. Paradigms are the glasses that one sees through which colour how and what we see. When they shift, so does the world. Today it's almost a cliché to speak about new paradigm shifts occurring. Paradigms are shifting kaleidoscopically these days. This makes sense in light of the fact that - according to the latest reports from quantum physicists - we inhabit a universe that is composed of undulating vibrations, oscillating in continuously and infinitely varied rhythms and frequencies. The universe is filled with ambiguity and mystery. It is a shifting cascade of relativistic perspectives, where nothing is really quite solid, and we exist as mostly empty space and waves of possible probabilities. Our beliefs are the brain's attempt to freeze the flow of matter and energy into fixed states, so we can grasp onto something familiar and tangible in a shifting sea too grand for us to ever fully comprehend. [3]

Mavericks are sometimes not 'politically correct' - especially when such 'correctness' is defined by people with power. The mavericks with a significant degree of togetherness (Jesus, Francis of Assisi et. al.) couldn't give a (stuff - or substitute your own term) about 'official' approval.

But the best mavericks are not afflicted with 'tunnel vision'. They are willing to tolerate ambiguity [4], and they enjoy diversity [5]. They believe, for example, that we live by the 'Holy Conjunction' - 'and'. As Scott Peck puts it somewhere in *In Search of Stones:* we affirm reason and emotion, reason and revelation - to which I would add science and faith, mind and heart (light and heat), spirit and word, tradition and renewal, order and freedom, conservatism and liberalism. (But re the latter: as someone has said, conservatives believe too much, liberals too little). There are six ways to worship in the Bible and today, not one. [6]. There are six broad answers to the question 'How do people get to know God?' [7]. There are at least five answers to the question 'How should the church be governed?' [8]. Let us resist the common temptation to separate what God has put together.

Yes, I like mavericks. Some, of course, are *idiots savants;* they're crazy. They believe they're the only ones in the regiment in step. But I admire genuine mavericks, and wish I had the courage of some of them. Like former Roman Catholic priest Philip Berrigan who has been arrested more than 100 times and spent more than six years behind bars.

And I confess to being a bit of a maverick. For example, like those 'IBM Fellows' I try to avoid attending committees. I used to tell groups of clergy 'I do everything a pastor does - preach, teach, counsel, marry, bury - but I attend few or no committees, nor do I organise anything'. The greenness of their envy was palpable! I was once interviewed for a senior position at a large

Christian organisation. Fortunately the CEO believed me when I said, 'I'll be of best help here if you keep me off committees.' (But some other senior executives could not understand this approach. 'How could someone who doesn't drive to the office in the city traffic and attend meetings be of benefit to us?'). At Melbourne's Blackburn Baptist Church in the 1970s, I mostly delegated committee-work to others, and spent each morning in prayer, writing and reading - and the church grew by 15% each year. In another church (where I lasted only nine months), staff-members complained that I was not in the church office all day like the previous pastor.

Management guru Peter Drucker believes churches spend ten times too much time in committees. I agree with him. [9]

Now, don't get me wrong. We need committees, and people to organise things. But I don't belong to those groups.

However, I don't want a 'maverick' managing my money at the bank; nor interpreting the law if ever I'm in trouble; nor reporting news-events. There's a case sometimes for non-creative conformism.

Mavericks have minority opinions on some things. For example, I have 'Rev.' in front of my name. What does that mean? Nothing much, really. I have been 'ordained' (a better word would be 'commissioned' or 'accredited') to a ministry of leadership in the Baptist churches of our nation (Australia). If I take all this more seriously than that, I believe I would be guilty of the heresy (that's the word, it's not a misprint) of 'clericalism'. Occasionally, I tell theological students that their abhorrence of clericalism will diminish when their denomination gives them a 'Rev.', and they're invited to enjoy privileged status in church forums. 'You should never use the word "minister" in the singular', I lecture, and they all nod vigorously. (They nod for other reasons when I talk about clericalism in clergy conferences.)

What does all that mean? Simply that the role of the 'clergy' is to empower the church for their ministry - not the other way around. [10]

Now where did I get this tendency towards nonconformity? It came to light in Spiritual Direction a couple of decades ago. My father never talked to me. So what, you may ask? Well, psychologists talk about transference or projection. I apparently projected onto other authority-figures some anger about my earliest authority-figure's preoccupation with other things.

Further: All institutions are inherently degenerative, according to sociologist Robert Merton. Or, to put it another way: the evil of institutions is generally greater than the sum of the evil of the individuals within them. Power corrupts, et *cetera*...

When I worked as an Intervarsity staff worker with tertiary students in the late 1960s, I felt good about their telegenic protests. Mind you, many might have been angry not only about Vietnam, but because they weren't breast-fed or something. They chose to be 'different in order to be difficult'. But some of their ideas proved to be prophetic.

I like the comment by our Australian former prime minister Malcolm Fraser. Writing about economic globalisation he says, 'The demonstrations against these changes before the world's financial meetings can't just be written down to some half-mad people who can't understand what is good for them. The growing inequality between rich and poor as individuals and as nations is unsustainable'. [11] Another prophetic idea.

The slogan about Christianity 'comforting the disturbed and disturbing the comfortable' was first suggested by G. K. Chesterton. Pastors, they say these days, comfort the disturbed (and will be disturbed themselves by powerful people if they in turn do too much disturbing). It's the prophet's task to disturb the comfortable (and prophets don't usually get an imprimatur from religious institutions for their ministry: how many second-plus generation churches can you name which commissions people to a truly 'prophetic' ministry?). Prophets make waves. They're gadflies. And even though they're always in the minority, they're sometimes right.

So be warned. As the saying attributed to Martin Niemoller puts it: 'First they came for the communists, but I was not a communist - so I said nothing. Then they came for the social democrats, but I was not a social democrat - so I did nothing. Then the trade unionists, but I was not a trade unionist. And then they came for the Jews, but I was not a Jew - so I did little. Then when they came for me, there was no one left who could stand up for me'.

Organisations need structure, rules, committees, precedents. But, as IBM learned, you need 'to combine the strengths of the organisation with the strengths of the independent operator'. The church too must wrestle with the challenge of encouraging the dreamer, learning from the heretic, tolerating the gadfly, and accommodating the maverick. It needs them as certainly as does IBM.' [12]

If you belong to a small group and want to talk further about all this, try the discussion starters here. [13].

In another chapter we'll look at Doubters. After that: 'How does one move from mere nonconformity or doubting to faith?'

Footnotes

[1] https://www.urbandictionary.com/define.php?term=Maverick

[2] M. Scott Peck, *In Search of Stones,* London: Simon & Schuster, 1995, p. 233.

[3] David Jay Brown and Rebecca McClen Novick, *Mavericks of the Mind: Conversations for the New Millennium,* (Crossing Press, 1993), from their Introduction. See http://www.levity.com/mavericks/frames10.htm

[4] http://www.jmm.org.au/articles/9289.htm

[5] http://www.jmm.org.au/articles/11365.htm

[6] http://www.jmm.org.au/articles/8736.htm

[7] See Richard Foster's book *Streams of Living Water* for a brilliant exposition of that idea

[8] Variously emphasised by Presbyterians ['elders'], Episcopalians ['bishops'], Baptists [the congregation], prophets and apostles.

[9] See here for some examples of Peter Drucker's maverick ideas -http://sourcesofinsight.com/lessons-learned-from-peter-drucker/

[10] See my 'Pastoral Survival Guide' for more: http://www.jmm.org.au/articles/8658.htm

[11] *The Melbourne Age* (28 December 2001)

[12] J. David Newman, Editorial, *Ministry,* May 1990, pp. 22-23.

[13] FOR FURTHER THOUGHT/DISCUSSION:

1. Jesus was regarded as a maverick by Pharisees, scribes and elders because he would not conform to their 'traditions'. What traditions today might Jesus have problems with?

2. Jesus was also regarded as a 'maverick' by the common people: he 'spoke with authority, not as the scribes'. How does a pastor/preacher/prophet get to be like that?
3. 'We nice people don't crucify prophets any more. We just don't invite them back.' True in your church?
4. Why is 'clericalism' a heresy?
5. Why do only a small minority of ex-heads of State (e.g. Jimmy Carter and Malcolm Fraser) speak up for the poor?
6. 'I always want to be somebody of independent thought. I don't want to be pushed into a corner by convention or by what people think' (Sir Peter Ustinov). Why is that rare?
7. From a document on Organisational Change: 'The human need to be accepted by a group - whether family, friends, co-workers or neighbours - gives the group leverage to demand compliance to its cultural norms. Even more so if the individual feels vulnerable, e.g. a new starter or promotion or transferee (changing levels or teams/departments, is usually accompanied by learning the cultural norms of the new group). Were such a need not so widespread, groups would have little hold on people other than formal sanctions. The nonconformists and mavericks who defy pressures to adhere to group norms always do so at a considerable risk and often pay a price!' How does that apply to your organisation/ church/es?
8. Thoreau talked about 'listening to the sound of a different drummer'. How can we encourage people who are different?

9. Think of some iconoclasts you know. Talk about their positive or negative contribution to others' thinking and behaviour.
10. A generation ago, a fashion designer preached that people should dress more casually. Now they do. He recently wrote: 'So, we have come to this: An idea that I touted for twenty years has become the vogue, and I will have to abandon it because it is against my principles to like fashionable things.' Can you think of other examples of notions that were once 'maverick' now being the norm?
11. 'When IT mavericks become angry, paranoid, or narcissistic, they create viruses.' Do they? Why?
12. Gavin *Ewart's sonnet Equality of the Sexes* suggests that nonconformists exist within both genders. Do they?
13. 'Managing an advertising agency isn't all beer and skittles. After fourteen years of it, I have come to the conclusion that the manager has one principal responsibility: to provide an atmosphere in which creative mavericks can do useful work.' (David Ogilvy) . How can a church provide an atmosphere for 'creative mavericks'?
14. McDonald's is 'successful' because, as founder Ray Kroc said: 'We will not tolerate nonconformists'. Writes one commentator: 'That, in many ways, still is the McDonald's corporate culture. Uniformity and conformity are crucial to the rise of the industry, and it is remarkable how they have achieved that. When I visited McDonald's in Dachau [Germany], it could have been Idaho. I could have been in Colorado. And

if you closed your eyes and tasted that hamburger, you could have been anywhere on the planet in a McDonald's. The food was exactly the same.' So...???

Chapter 3
TED Talk: LET'S MAKE IT SIMPLE - WHAT WOULD JESUS DO?

> *Preachers could learn from TED/TEDx talks. Their motto: 'ideas-worth-spreading'. The world's leading 'thinkers and doers' – like Bill Gates and Richard Branson, and hundreds of others – speak for 18 minutes or less. The talks are then posted daily, free, on TED.com – or you can follow them on Twitter and Facebook.*
>
> *These speakers share their ideas about how to change the world. They invite us to 'step out of our habitual path of thinking...'*

Here's my TEDx talk if ever I was invited to give one:

WHAT WOULD JESUS DO?

If I were to choose one person to follow as a mentor/guide, the best human being I've ever heard of is Jesus of Nazareth. If I find a better-put-together person, I promise you, I'll switch allegiance to them.

When I talk about Jesus to people, I often get 'Yes but' responses. A common one: 'Yes, but, you've got faith, I haven't.'

How do you usually travel? Car? Tram? Train? How many of you stopped and thought, 'Do I have enough faith to get into/onto this thing?' Maybe if your car has let you down, that might be a possibility but what you've thought about is actually not your faith as such, but its object. Same with people. Is this car reliable? Is this person reliable?

So why do people have faith in an ancient historical figure like Jesus? My grandmother heard a voice – a real voice, she says – in the night. I never have. The great St Augustine heard a child's voice, and 'all the shadows of doubt were dispelled'. Saul of Tarsus had a Damascus Road experience – with a blinding light and a voice from the sky. In a life-changing experience of surrender to God, C. S. Lewis knelt and prayed in his room at Magdalen College, Oxford – 'perhaps that night the most dejected and reluctant convert in all England'. Nothing like that's ever happened to me.

So why is Jesus important to me? I didn't commit myself to him because of a theological system, or even church services. I didn't follow him because my parents did: as I started thinking for myself, I rejected their simplistic fundamentalism in many respects.

My 'conversion' really happened when I left home and started reading and thinking about this amazing person who, on about eighty occasions in the Gospels, went around speaking and acting as if he were an emissary from God. Imagine if you heard someone in Melbourne's Flinders Street saying to strangers he'd just met, 'I forgive your sins. It doesn't matter who you committed them against, I forgive you!' You'd probably be both perplexed and a bit scared – and maybe you'd phone our country's emergency number, OOO.

If what this Jew claimed about himself were true, then it's all really breath-taking: he embodied 'the hopes and fears of all the years' for his people if only they'd realised it...

Now if eye-witnesses claimed someone you'd never actually met was the Son of God, what are we to make of that?

A.

I reckon there are only four possibilities:
- Perhaps he was mad. I once met a psychotic person in a psychiatric hospital who claimed to be God. Problem was on that day he was Napoleon Bonaparte, and sometimes he's the

man in the moon. Was Jesus one of those? No: he's the sanest person I've ever heard of.
- Was he a liar, an imposter? Problem with that is the question 'What did he have to gain by it all?' And what kind of person was Jesus on the evil-to-goodness spectrum? I think the question answers itself.
- Was he, then, a good person, a great teacher, and that's all? C. S. Lewis wrote about this 'patronising nonsense about his being a great human teacher... He has not left that open to us. He did not intend to.'
- So, did his followers get it wrong? And to a person they were prepared to die for something they'd concocted? I for one find that less credible than believing they reported Jesus' words and actions truthfully, and eventually came to believe in him.

ooOoo

So, you ask, of all the people who've claimed a special relationship with God, only one was right? Yes. If Jesus was God's Son, a lot follows: He was the 'Word' by whom the universe was created, says John the evangelist. He is 'who you need'.

And then there's his death on a cross. The 19th century German philosopher Nietzsche ridiculed the idea of [Divinity] on a cross. But as John Stott writes, 'When he was spread-eagled and skewered on his cross, strung up with nails or ropes or both, what looked like the defeat of goodness by evil was really the defeat of evil by goodness.' [1]

I once heard with astonishment my English professor – an atheist – say that all great operas and literature are essentially about one or more of three core human experiences – guilt, love and death. That was an 'aha' experience for me: the cross of

Christ was about all three, the theologians tell us. [2]

I remember talking to that professor about who Jesus might be and went through the classical 'quadrilemma' I referred to a couple of minutes ago. Does all that make sense? I asked him. 'Yeah'. But you're not a Christian? 'No'. May I ask why not? He said it had little to do with logic, but rather lifestyle. He enjoyed living life his way, without being answerable to any God. Fairly common, I would think. C. S. Lewis in his autobiography *Surprised by Joy* put it well: 'When I examined myself I found [within me] a zoo of lusts, a bedlam of ambitions, a nursery of fears, a harem of fondled hatreds...' [3]

That's the first of two big questions: the issue of faith, and its cousin, intellectual credibility. If Jesus is the Divine Son of God, he has a right to demand allegiance.

B.

So what's he asking us to do? Simple: 'Follow me.'

What does that mean? In the Gospel of John, he gives his followers a mandate: 'As the Father has sent me, so I'm sending you' (John 20:21). In other words: what you have seen me do, you do!

What's that? At the beginning of Jesus' public ministry (Luke 4:18), he gives us a dot-point summary: he came to offer 'Good news to the poor, freedom for captives, sight for the blind, to set the oppressed free, and to release people from their debts.' Whatever inhibits our well-being, Jesus offers to bring healing in those areas...

And that's what we're to do. Indeed, at the final judgment (Matthew 25:37-38), we'll be asked how we went with all that. Jesus today is hungry needing food; thirsty, needing clean water; a stranger needing our hospitality; or naked needing clothes; sick, or in prison, needing our help...

SO... WHAT DO WE DO, AND WHERE DO WE START?

1. We begin with a commitment to follow Jesus. We invite Jesus into our life, and Jesus' Spirit helps sort us out in terms of the collected baggage, guilt and shame that's accumulated there.
2. And our motto, our watch-word, is the same as Jesus' Great Commandment: 'You shall love the Lord your God with all your heart, mind, soul and strength, and your neighbour as yourself' (Luke 10:27-28). Jesus' hearers had a 'Yes, but' question about that: 'Who is my neighbour?' Not easy.
   When Serbs are slaughtering Muslims, who is my neighbour? When Tutsis are being killed by Hutus, who is my neighbour? When hundreds of thousands are being slaughtered by radical Islamists in Syria and Iraq, who is my neighbour? Jesus' parable of the Good Samaritan answers this very clearly: my neighbour is someone – anyone – who needs my help and I'm in a position to offer it.
3. And before we rush off to help everyone, and in the process get 'spattered all over the wall of needfulness' we do what Jesus suggested when the needs are so numerous and so great: 'The harvest is plentiful...' so – what? PRAY (Luke 10:2).
4. And prayer is so important that we develop a relationship in the stillness and quietness of a 'desert' rather than rushing around wearing ourselves out. Speaking of TED talks, I note this week that there's one titled 'We're all trying to be multi-taskers. It's good for nothing!' All of God's best leaders, best people, regularly spend time in deserts, as Jesus did.

5. Then – LISTEN. 'A true friend is someone who listens to you and to God at the same time.' But don't get too addicted to 'helping' others. I've met many people who get a 'buzz' out of needing to be needed... Thoreau suggested 'If you see someone coming towards you with the obvious intent of doing you good, run for your life'. Or C. S. Lewis: 'She went around doing good: you could tell those she want to help by their hunted look!'
6. Work with others to alleviate the needs of the marginalised. Dave Andrews tells a terrific story about some squatters in Brisbane who were constantly harassed by the police. Because they camped illegally, of course the police had to keep moving them on. Solution: 'Bricks through the police station windows'. Dave had another suggestion: invite the police for coffee, and talk about it. Eventually the Council and State Government found some ways to accommodate these homeless people legally. [4]

Dave signed his book when he kindly gave me a copy: 'To Rowland Croucher, with the prayer that you will not only keep the faith, but also the love that is at the heart of our faith'.

7. And, if you're able, speak truth to power. Jesus did this especially with the Jewish religious and political authorities (though some have thought he was a bit soft on Rome... but that's a discussion for another day). An excellent book to whet your appetite: Peter McKinnon's *The Songs of Jesse Adams* - about what Jesus might have done if he were to come to Melbourne a generation ago. [5]

Conclusion: So doing what Jesus did helps answer the greatest existential questions I face about my life: Who am I? Do I have worth? What am I supposed to be doing with the one life I'm given?

It's simple, really: Follow Jesus. Do what Jesus did. If you try to 'save your life' you'll lose it. John Stott, one of my mentors, puts it like this: 'If you insist on living for yourself, you'll lose yourself. But if you're prepared to lose yourself and give yourself away in love for God and your fellow human beings, then in that moment of complete abandon, when you think you have lost everything, the miracle happens and you find yourself'. [6]

And St Paul's excellent summary:

> *So this is my prayer: that your love will flourish and that you will not only love much but well. Learn to love appropriately. You need to use your head and test your feelings so that your love is sincere and intelligent, not sentimental gush. Live a lover's life, circumspect and exemplary, a life Jesus will be proud of: bountiful in fruits from the soul, making Jesus Christ attractive to all, getting everyone involved in the glory and praise of God. (Philippians 1:9-11).*

(Taken from a sermon preached at St Martins' Collingwood in 2014 and in many other places.)

Footnotes

[1] John Stott, *Why I am a Christian,* (IVP, 2013), p. 61.
[2] For example, Gustav Aulen in *Christus Victor.*
[3] C. S. Lewis, *Surprised by Joy* (*Geoffrey Bles*, 1955), p. 143.
[4] Dave Andrews, *Can You Hear the Heartbeat: A Challenge to Care the Way Jesus Cared* (Hodder and Stoughton 1989) pp. 112ff. Dave was in the media recently because of his excellent ministry 'Befriending Muslims'.
[5] Peter McKinnon, *The Songs of Jesse Adams,* (Acorn 2014). For my review, visit http://www.jmm.org.au/articles/33782.htm
[6] John Stott, *Why I am a Christian*, 2013, p. 97.

Chapter 4
JESUS' 'KEY TO UNDERSTANDING': LOVE

> *I once asked my Facebook friends: 'What was Jesus' "KEY TO KNOWLEDGE/ UNDERSTANDING"? (Luke 11:52: "Woe to you lawyers! For you have taken away the key of knowledge; you did not enter yourselves, and you hindered those who were entering.")'* [1]

Must be something pretty important...
I posted these questions: 'What is it? Ever heard a sermon on this?'
If I recall correctly, no one had...
Which is very, very odd.

If Jesus is saying something to religious leaders about what we might call these days 'A Theory of Everything', I for one want to know what he's talking about.

The best summary is ten verses back: Luke 11:42 'But woe to you Pharisees! For you tithe mint and rue and herbs of all kinds, and neglect justice and the love of God; it is these you ought to have practised, without neglecting the others.'

On another occasion a Pharisee who was a lawyer, asked Jesus, 'Teacher, which commandment in the law is the greatest?' Jesus said to him, "You shall love the Lord your God with all your heart, and with all your soul, and with all your mind." This is the greatest and first commandment. And a second is like it: "You shall love your neighbour as yourself." On these two commandments hang all the law and the prophets.' (Matthew 22:36-40).

So there are Jesus' headlines: Justice and love (P.S. You won't find them headlined - or even mentioned - in the classical Christian creeds).

Let's look at love first.

THE MEANING OF LOVE

Our English language uses the one word 'love' to mean several things: romantic love, family love, 'brotherly/sisterly' love, and self-sacrificing (*agape*) love. The Greek word *agape* refers to the distinctive Christian way to love.

It's indiscriminate: we are to love others with *agape* love whether they are fellow believers (John 13:34) or bitter enemies (Matthew 5:44).

Jesus' parable of the Good Samaritan is all about sacrifice for the sake of others, even for those who may belong to a group we regard as enemies.

As modelled by Christ, genuine love is not based on feelings; it is an act of the will, putting the well-being of others above our own. The best description of *agape* love is in 1 Corinthians 13 (why not Google it?). God loves like this. God doesn't discriminate between those who 'deserve' to be loved and others we regard as 'unlovable'.

The most graphic example of *agape* love in the New Testament centres on the cross: 'While we were still sinners, Christ died for us' (Romans 5:8). Richard Rohr: 'What kind of God would submit to being strung up naked on a cross?'

Agape love does not come naturally to us. We have a tendency to love those we like, or who like us.

A basic Christian doctrine asserts that if we are to love as God loves, that love can only come from its Source. This is the love that 'has been poured out into our hearts through the Holy Spirit, who has been given to us' (Romans 5:5; cf. Galatians 5:22). 'This is how we know what love is: Jesus Christ laid down his life for us. And we ought to lay down our lives for our brothers and sisters' (1 John 3:16).

LOVE FOR THE WORLD

'We in Australia have retreated into a delusionary mental bubble where self-interest is a prime motivator', says Tim Costello, the chief advocate of World Vision Australia. He cites the slashing of Australia's foreign aid budget - then 0.22% of Gross National Income (a global measure of donor generosity) in 2017-18, the lowest level in Australia's history. [2]

Sadly, my country Australia has taken a hard line against the 2000+ asylum-seekers classified as 'illegal maritime arrivals', and to dissuade others from coming by boat, we spend $1 billion per year locking them away on Manus Island (Papua New Guinea) and another off-shore island, Nauru. They mostly came from Iran, Sri Lanka, Pakistan, Bangladesh, Afghanistan, Iraq (and also include nearly 200 stateless asylum seekers). Whilst travel advice to the rest of us is to exercise a 'high degree of caution' if we must travel to those countries, our message to asylum seekers from these places is to 'Take the package, and go back to your country of origin!'

Something doesn't quite add up there, particularly as we also factor in the emotional trauma we've caused by locking those people up. A little voice in our heads is saying 'It's a form of torture to punish one group of people to dissuade others...' Discuss with your family/friends: what's the loving thing to do in this situation?

SO HOW CAN I BE MORE LOVING?

In *Twelve Steps to a Compassionate Life* [3], Karen Armstrong offers these suggestions from mainly Christian and Buddhist traditions. She suggests spending a week on each:

1. **Learn About Compassion:** It's not simply a list of directives. A pagan approached Rabbi Hillel and promised to convert to Judaism if he could recite the entire Torah while he stood on one leg. Hillel replied, 'What is hateful to yourself do not to [others]. That is the whole of the Torah and the remainder is but commentary.'
2. **Look at Your Own World.** Armstrong suggests that we think in terms of the Confucian concentric circles of compassion, starting with your family, moving to friends and community, and finally to the country in which you live. For example: what can you do to make each family member valued? Then, ditto those with whom you work. And so on...
3. **Compassion for Yourself.** The late rabbi Albert Friedlander, who grew up in Nazi Germany was bewildered by the vicious anti-Semitic propaganda back then. 'One night, when he was about eight years old, he deliberately lay awake and made a list of all his good qualities... Finally, he vowed that if he survived, he would use those qualities to build a better world.'
4. **Empathy.** Our negative or difficult life-experiences can help us understand the sufferings of others. The young lawyer Gandhi was tossed off a train in South Africa because 'coloured' people weren't permitted to travel first class. This experience coloured the rest of his life in terms of nonviolent resistance to oppression.

5. **Mindfulness.** 'In mindfulness we mentally stand back and observe our behaviour while we are engaged in the normal processes of living in order to discover more about the way we interact with people, what makes us angry and unhappy, how to analyse our experiences, and how to pay attention to the present moment... Mindfulness, over time, [teaches us] how often the real cause of our suffering is the anger that resides within us.'
6. **Action.** Let us create 'spots of time' for other people when we show 'little, nameless, unremembered, acts of kindness and love'. And, conversely, remember the unkind remarks – whether you were the giver or receiver – that have been a corrosive presence in your life or in the lives of others.
7. **How Little We Know.** 'Religion is at its best when it helps us to ask questions and holds us in a state of wonder – and arguably as its worst when it tries to answer them authoritatively and dogmatically... Transcendence... lies beyond the reach of the senses, and is therefore incapable of definitive proof...'
8. **How Should We Speak to One Another?** Unfortunately the language of politics is mostly too aggressive, and destroys the quest for humble compassion, arousing passions that are already bitter and entrenched. Do we want to win the argument or seek the truth? And let us also 'hear what is not uttered aloud. Angry speech in particular requires careful decoding. Make an effort to hear the pain or fear that surfaces in body language, tone of voice, and choice of imagery'.
9. **Concern for Everybody.** In theory, all religions affirm that compassion cannot be confined to our own group.

We must reach out in some way to the stranger and the foreigner – even to the enemy. 'If we continue to make our national interest an absolute value, to see our cultural heritage and way of life as supreme, and to regard outsiders and foreigners with suspicion and neglect their interests, the interconnected global society we have created will not be viable. After the world wars, genocide, and terrorism of the twentieth century, the purpose of the tribe or the nation can no longer be to fight, dominate, exploit, conquer, colonise, occupy, kill, convert, or terrorise rival groups. We have a duty to get to know one another, and to cultivate a concern and responsibility for all our neighbours in the global village.... Understanding different national, cultural, and religious traditions is no longer a luxury; it is now a necessity and must become a priority.'

10. **Knowledge.** Karen Armstrong says that deciphering the cultural, religious, and political customs of other peoples requires more time and energy than most people are willing to expend. But, she says, 'We owe it to our nation and to others to develop a wider, more pan-optic knowledge and understanding of our neighbours'.

Often, we are so imbued with our own tribal prejudices that we criticise others for behaviours that we have been guilty of. '(Even-mindedness) presupposes an awareness of prejudices, preconceptions, attachments, and blind spots that can cloud our understanding. We are striving for an equability that can look at world problems without undue attachment to our national self-interest and that can transcend religious or cultural chauvinism in an appreciation of others.' 'When Wilfred Cantwell Smith

(1916-2000)...was teaching Islamic studies at McGill University, he used to make his students observe the fast during Ramadan, celebrate Islamic holidays, and perform the prayers at the correct time – even to get up for the dawn prayer – because he was convinced that it was impossible to understand another faith simply by reading books about it.'

11. **Recognition.** Karen Armstrong tells a compelling story from Irishwoman Christina Noble's biography, *Bridge Across My Sorrows*. 'At a very unhappy time of her life, Christina Noble had a powerful dream: "Naked children were running down a dirt road fleeing from napalm bombing... one of the girls had a look in her eyes that implored me to pick her up and protect her and take her to safety. Above the escaping children was a brilliant white light that contained the word 'Vietnam'. From that moment, Christina was convinced, in a way she could not understand, that it was her destiny to go to Vietnam and that one day she would work with children there.' The eventual result: She went to Vietnam to rescue street children, and set up the Children's Medical and Social Centre in Ho Chi Minh City in 1991. There now are foundations in France, the United States, and Australia. 'Christina found that the way to transcend the overwhelming memories of her appalling childhood in Dublin was to work practically to alleviate the pain of others.'

12. **Love Your Enemies.** Gandhi said, 'An eye for an eye makes the whole world blind'. Karen Armstrong says, 'We [must] learn to appreciate the wisdom of restraint toward the enemy'.

Gandhi again: 'Mine is not an exclusive love. I cannot love Moslems or Hindus and hate Englishmen. For if I love merely Hindus and Moslems because their ways are on the whole pleasing to me, I shall soon begin to hate them when their ways displease me, as they may well do at any moment. A love that is based on the goodness of those whom you love is a mercenary affair'.

Karen Armstrong also cites Nelson Mandela, who 'without any feelings of recrimination... walked out of the South African prison in which he had been confined for twenty-seven years, and when he came to power initiated a process of reconciliation rather than seeking revenge'.

Then there's the Dalai Lama who has renounced vengefulness, refusing to condemn the Chinese even though they destroyed his monasteries and massacred his monks...

Martin Luther King, Jr. believed the highest point in Jesus' life was the moment he forgave his executioners, when instead of attempting to defeat evil with evil, he was able to prevail over it with good: 'Only goodness can drive out evil and only love can overcome hate'.

'In our global village', Karen Armstrong concludes, 'everybody is our neighbour, and it is essential to make allies of our enemies. We need to create a world democracy in which everybody's voice is heard and everybody's aspirations are taken seriously. In the last resort, this kind of 'love' and 'concern for everybody' will serve our best interest better than short-sighted and self-serving policies.'

ooOoo

In the next chapter, we explore the notion of Social Justice, which Jesus actually mentioned before love (Matthew 23:23, Luke 11:42).

Footnotes

[1] Luke 11:52 NRSV. Unless otherwise noted we'll use the *New Revised Standard Version* (NRSV) translation of the Bible: it has a worldwide reputation among biblical scholars for its accuracy and clarity. Occasionally I may cite Eugene Peterson's racy *The Message* translation, which is closest to modern - particularly American - idioms.

[2] Wikipedia's list of Development Aid Country Donors puts Australia, in 2015, 16th in the world in terms of its percentage, then 0.27%, of gross national income. America's? 0.17%. The UN's target is 0.7%!

[3] Karen Armstrong, *Twelve Steps to a Compassionate Life* (Bodley Head, London, 2011). I am indebted to the following article for help with this summary of Karen Armstrong's wisdom:
https://compassionatews.wordpress.com/.../12-steps-to-a-comp.../

Chapter 5
SOCIAL JUSTICE (1)
HOW TO KNOW THE LORD –
WHAT IS SOCIAL JUSTICE?

As long as poverty, injustice and gross inequality persist in our world, none of us can truly rest. (Nelson Mandela)

Extreme poverty anywhere is a threat to human security everywhere. (Kofi Annan, Seventh Secretary-General of the UN)

Poverty is the worst form of violence. (Mahatma Gandhi)

Poverty is like punishment for a crime you didn't commit. (Eli Khamarov)

'Justice and righteousness... Caring for the poor and needy ... Is not this to know me? says the Lord.' Jeremiah 22:15b-16

Christians of all kinds – Catholic, Conciliar and Evangelical – are now more concerned than ever about social justice. Theology is never a 'value-free' discipline, and in a world of stark injustices, many are doing theology from the side of the poor, rather than from an acquiescent, privatised Western perspective.

For CATHOLICS, *Mater et Magistra* (1961) broke the long alliance between Catholicism and socially conservative forces. Twenty years later, *Laborem Exercens* inveighed against multinationals fixing high prices for their products and very low prices for raw materials.

EVANGELICALS in Berlin (1966) asserted that 'social involvement' was the enemy of 'biblical evangelism'; Lausanne (1974) viewed them as complementary; Wheaton (1983) saw social action and political engagement as integral to evangelism. And the *Manila Manifesto* (1989) said most clearly: 'We affirm that we must demonstrate God's love visibly by caring for those who are deprived of justice, dignity, food, and shelter'.

The World Council of Churches' *Towards a Church in Solidarity with the Poor* (1980) urges us to read the Bible from the perspective of the poor: 'The Bible is a book of hope, concern and solidarity with the poor .... Unfortunately when the poor were given low priority in the life of the churches... ecclesiastical institutions frequently become part of oppressive systems'.

Who am I to write on this subject? I belong to the group least qualified to speak about justice and the poor. I am a white, Anglo-Saxon ('Progressive') Evangelical, middle-class, a 'senior citizen', well-educated, living in a rich, lucky country (Australia) with a happy family in a quiet, treed suburb. I can 'work' most systems to my advantage. My ministry is fulfilling, I'm on a seniors' pension, I've been around the world several times. I've worked hard, saved hard, studied hard, and I play hard. As a kid, I scrounged bottles, animal manure and scrap metal for pocket money. We were not rich, but we were never hungry.

I grew up believing most of the poor were either lazy or stupid. Why the constant shortage of bricklayers? If Japan can do it, why not Bangladesh?

Righteous indignation focused on things like pornography, violence and sexual sins, rarely such macro-ethical issues as poverty, injustice, race and war.

My 'conversion' began when I found that most of those who served the poor did not share these ideas. Dom Helder Camara, for example, flirted with fascism ('God, Fatherland and Family', 'order is more important than justice') until he worked in the favelas in Rio – those festering piles of human beings separated by bits of cardboard and corrugated iron. [1]

Paulo Freire says the middle class has a choice – to identify with the rich and influential, or with the poor, who have very few choices.

The income gap between the poor and the rich, everywhere, is widening. Since the Industrial Revolution we've never learned to share wealth properly. It's not 'trickling down' to the ever-increasing poor.

THE BIBLE is certainly big on justice. The Hebrew and Greek words for justice (*tzedek* and *dikaiosune*) may have three meanings: personal virtue (Noah, or Joseph, were 'just' - Genesis 6:9, Matthew 1:19); judicial fairness (Leviticus 19) or social responsibility: behaviour towards others which is like a covenant God's gracious concern for us. Unfortunately, the King James Version's use of 'righteousness' for *tzedek* gives the impression, not of justice, but rather holiness of living, which is an important but diminished understanding of the biblical idea.

Social justice concerns attitudes to the least privileged – the poor, widows, orphans, foreigners. When harvesting, the Israelites were to leave them something (Deuteronomy 24:19-21). Interest on loans is forbidden (Exodus 22:25). Slaves must not be treated harshly (Leviticus 25:39-43). There is a clear relationship between oppression and poverty: 'Remember you were once slaves' (Deuteronomy 26:5-8). The God of the Exodus intervenes on behalf of the powerless and oppressed: so must God's people.

The message of the Hebrew prophets: Seek justice, correct oppression (Isaiah 1:17). They thunder against the rich and powerful who oppress the poor but their outrage is strongest against a religion devoid of justice (Hosea 6:6, 8:13; Amos 5:15, 21-25; Micah 6:6-8, Isaiah 58:1-11; cf. Proverbs 21:3). God accepts or rejects Israel's worship according to their concern for the poor. Even prayer mustn't be a substitute for helping the poor (Isaiah 1:15-17). In the relatively affluent 8th century BCE Israel, poverty was not accidental. The prosperity of the rich rested largely on the exploitation and mistreatment of the poor – through a legal system biased towards the rich, monopoly control, restrictive trade practices, unjust wages and arbitrary price increases. Many of the poor had lost their land to large property owners: later, Ezekiel rebukes the rich for unscrupulously accumulating real estate for profit (22:28).

Many of the Psalms describe God judging the world with justice. 'The Lord executes justice for the oppressed'. [2]

Mary's *Magnificat* praises a God who shows mercy, scatters the proud, puts down the mighty, lifts up the lowly, feeds the hungry (Luke 1:46-55).

Jesus' ministry will bring good news to the poor ... announces a 'jubilee' (Luke 4:16-19). In the Jubilee (Leviticus 25:3-5, 8-12), soil was to be left fallow, debts remitted, slaves liberated, and property returned to owners who had forfeited it by debt.

God in Christ becomes poor, choosing the weak, as Paul says, to 'confound the mighty'. The Kingdom, says Jesus, is given to the poor (and to the rich if they will repent). It is all about new relationships – with God, with others. It turns our customary values upside down: so the 'first in the kingdom' are those with no status in society. The poor are blessed, not because of their poverty and misery, nor because they are 'better' than others but because they recognise their need for God (Matthew 11:5, 5:3-11, Luke 6:20). To the rich, the gospel is 'bad news before it is good news', so the rich young ruler, with his inordinate love of money and power is told to sell his possessions and give them to the poor so that he could have 'treasure in heaven' (Matthew 19:16-30). No wonder the poor, the outcasts, the 'excluded' heard Jesus gladly. He enjoyed parties with disreputables, so the religious establishment was outraged at his behaviour.

Jesus cut across selfish patriotisms and universalised the idea of 'neighbour'. Injustice done to anyone, anywhere, should be my concern. At the great judgment (Matthew 25:31-46) we shall learn that to serve others in their need is to serve the Lord himself. To ignore the poor is to turn away from the Lord. To be persecuted for the sake of justice is to be persecuted for the sake of Jesus (Matthew 5:6,10,11).

The New Testament epistles are replete with admonitions to care for the poor (e.g. Galatians 2:10, James 2:5-7, 5:1-6, 1 John 3:17, 1 Timothy 6:17-19). Greed is a cardinal sin, a form of idolatry (1 Corinthians 5:10-11, 6:10, Ephesians 4:19, 5:3,5, Colossians 3:5).

The Bible does not condemn inequality of possessions *per se*. Redistribution so that 'all have an equal share' is not a biblical idea. Those who argue this way will have to do it on philosophical or socio-political rather than biblical grounds. (Jesus enjoyed Galilee's feasting and suffered Golgotha's thirst. Paul experienced both prosperity and poverty, Philippians 4:12). What the Bible condemns is indifference by the affluent to the plight of the destitute. We 'bless the poor', not paternalistically, but as God has blessed us – 'grace justice' rather than 'parity justice'. The goal of justice is not equality, but *shalom*, a peace that assures the true humanity of individuals and communities.

A THEOLOGY OF SOCIAL JUSTICE

... must include the following:

* Every human being is made in God's image. (So we uphold the right of every person to live in freedom, in dignity, in peace, in health, and to know the One whom to know is to experience fullness of life.)
* Our generous Creator has entrusted us with a bountiful world, which we 'subdue' but also 'replenish'. The earth was given to all, not just to the rich. (There is enough food to go around – for our need, but not our greed. It is not God's will that a quarter of us live in luxury while the rest struggle to survive.)
* I am my brother's keeper. (I must not walk by on the other side of the road/tracks/sea.)
* God comes among us both as judge and victim (rebuking our selfishness and being nailed to a cross).
* We pray 'Give us this day our daily bread'. (If I am hungry, that is a material problem; if someone else is hungry, that is a spiritual problem – Berdyaev). So what can I, with limited resources, do about alleviating others' poverty?

We look at some practical responses in the next chapter.

Footnotes

[1] See chapter 7.
[2] e.g. Psalm 96:13; cf. 97:6, 98:9, 146:7.

Chapter 6
SOCIAL JUSTICE [2]
DOING JUSTICE - SO WHERE DO WE BEGIN?

'The really important teachings of the Law (are) justice and mercy and faith. These you should practise....'
(Matthew 23:23)

(1) RESEARCH: GET THE FACTS.

Talk to the "poor" – single parents, unemployed, migrants/refugees, anyone who feels marginalised – and to social workers, district nurses, mental health workers, etc.

Who are the poor? Definitions are elusive, but the poor know who they are. They have no 'place'. Some are poor geographically, 'displaced'. Others are poor emotionally, with no place in a loving family/community. Others are poor spiritually. Many are materially poor – they are deprived, within their communities, of the basic necessities to 'live decently'. In Australia, they may not be starving, but they can't afford a good education or holidays, or car repairs, or all the bills, especially rent (so we currently have an epidemic of 'couch surfing').

Why are they poor? Is it their own fault? Most answers are either too simple or untrue. Perhaps it's the death of a parent, ill-health, physical/mental disability, collapse of a business, breakdown of a marriage, lack of basic education, medical bills for sick children – the list is endless. As someone wisely put it: '....the causes of poverty are precipitated more by problems in the organisation and structures of society than by individuals themselves'.

Which brings us to economics. Our national and international systems revolve around greed and power – 'the international imperialism of money' (Pope Paul VI). People are rich or poor because of the 'distribution system'; what makes money gets done; what doesn't make money doesn't get done. Richard Nixon, when US president said in a moment of candour, 'The main purpose of American aid is not to help other nations, but to help ourselves.' (The current US president, Donald Trump, loudly agrees!)

Your morning cup of coffee: it's grown in the two-thirds world, where people are hungry. We have money for coffee while people in Sao Paulo's favelas have little or no money for food. So the plantation owners grow coffee for us instead of black beans for them. (It's the same with tobacco: and, incidentally, if you smoke and drink coffee you are forty times more likely to get lung cancer than if you imbibe neither). [1]

Heard of Minimata disease? A company in Japan - from 1932 to 1968 - kept dumping mercury into the water for years even after knowing it was causing paralysis, retardation, insanity and death. The company was simply making money. There's money in mercury poisoning, red dye #2, fluorocarbons, alcohol, tobacco, and a million other harmful things. [2] Big tobacco companies are increasingly targeting young smokers in the developing world (despite the 2005 international treaty which 168 nations signed banning aggressive tobacco advertising). [3]

Thousands of Australian households each year have their gas and electricity disconnected: many others go hungry to avoid this (they choose hunger to being cold). Foodbank, Australia's largest food relief organisation provides (2016) 60 million meals a year to over 2,400 charities. Last year, they distributed 33 million kilos of food and groceries with a retail value of more than $200 million. That's the equivalent of 166,000 meals a day. [4]

What are the functions of poverty? Peter le Breton and others offer lists like this one:

1. Dirty, repetitive, dangerous, undignified and menial work is done (mostly for low pay).
2. The rich can divert a higher proportion of income to savings and investment, to foster economic growth the benefits of which mostly favour the rich.
3. If you're rich enough you'll pay little or no tax: the tax burden falls unequally on poorer wage-earners.
4. The poor buy goods no one else wants – second-hand cars, clothes, etc. – enhancing incomes for sellers of these commodities.
5. Those who espouse social norms of the desirability of hard work and thrift can accuse others of being lazy and spendthrift. So these latter are, of course, undeserving of the privileges the former enjoy.
6. The deserving poor (e.g. the disabled) can allow the rest of us to feel altruistic, moral and practise the Judaeo-Christian ethic.
7. The powerless absorb the economic and social costs of change and growth: they are pushed out of their communities by high rents, urban 'development' and freeways to convey the middle-class from the suburbs to the central business district ... [5]

For Jesus, when a system got in the way of people's wholeness, it had to go. Inveighing against the Pharisees' legalistic religious system, he said, 'The sabbath was made for humans, not humans for the sabbath' (Mark

2:27). Our systems are mostly serving mammon, so we too will call for systemic change. We may not hold to any particular economic/political theory: a Christian is called to critique all ideologies. (As a cynic put it, capitalism is humans exploiting their fellow-humans; with communism it was the other way around!!).

(2) REFLECTION: THINK ABOUT THE FACTS.

Working hard to think clearly is the beginning of moral conduct (Pascal). Reflection and praxis go together. If one is sacrificed, the other suffers (Freire).

Beware of temptations not to think objectively. Our church congregations are mostly embedded in the rich half of society, so our 'suburban captivity' can be self-protective. We may meet few destitute 'hidden people'.

The problems are complex, but some things can be said simply:

1. Poverty is not just a lack of resources, but of power, of knowledge, of help and of hope. Poverty is loneliness. So it's not alleviated by handouts alone, but when the poor themselves become givers.

2. Reinhold Neibuhr has argued (convincingly in my view, in *Moral Man and Immoral Society*) that if we wait for the powerful to become altruistic we will wait forever. Power corrupts, and absolute power corrupts absolutely. The powerful have never – well, hardly ever – relinquished their privileges without some form of coercion being applied to them.

3. Let us beware of 'selective indignation', preaching only against evils threatening my family/group. Ask what Jesus got mad about...

4. Our education system encourages us to 'succeed' – which may not be the same as enhancing good human relationships. There's a tension in education between conformity to and the transformation of society. Some education may aim at collecting knowledge and degrees; transformation means asking how education can be liberating. (In Latin America learning to read is more than learning a skill, as in the West. It's a revolutionary activity as people learn about values and rights. We're also hearing liberated women in/from places like Pakistan and Afghanistan speaking like this).

5. Each of the world's peoples has its own particular cultural, ethnic and political distinctives: these must be respected. 'First world' models of development may not be appropriate to developing countries. In the film *Gandhi* I remember that great man saying to the British, 'Let us fail, if necessary, but with dignity, rather than have you here running things better while we are deprived of our liberty'. The 'excluded' must become the subjects of their own history, being part of the decision-making, and encouraged to control their own destinies.

6. 'You can't legislate morality' is a cop-out. All that is legislated is morality: the question is 'What kind?' When the state fails to legislate mercifully, we'll call the state to account, as the prophets did.

7. Jesus grew up in an oppressed country. The Zealots were 'freedom fighters', Herodians and Sadducees went along with the status quo; Essenes withdrew to the desert; Pharisees debated questions of private morality. Jesus disappointed them all, renouncing violence, exploitation, apathy and moralism: they're all dehumanising. His was the way of sacrificial love. [6]

(3) PRAY

Ask 'Who are my people? then pray fervently for them – and their oppressors. Prayer, says Jacques Ellul (*Prayer* and *Modern Man*) is the ultimate act of hope. Prayer rescues action from activism, and inaction from despair. But prayer is not a substitute for action. Contemplative love is not the end, but a means to the end of authentic love. As Thomas Merton put it: let us not forget that Mary and Martha are sisters.

(4) FEEL

This is 'listening presence', compassion, identification and encounter. We won't do this as well as Jesus did but we must try. We must not act for others merely through feelings of personal outrage, but when – and until – through caring friendship we earn the right to be invited to be their helper or advocate. Such feeling presence enables us to transcend narrow bigotries. Our practical help and advocacy for the poor will have the marks of suffering – the beatings, crown of thorns, and the nails – if we are truly following Christ.

(5) ACT CREATIVELY

We must do theology, not just be committed to reflection on reflection.

Let us not ever be overwhelmed by the magnitude of the problems: if enough individuals act, in concert, almost any problem can be solved. Robbers move against their victim; the priest and Levite have a passive mind-set and move away – to be 'neutral' (encouraging more injustice); the Good Samaritan uses the materials at his disposal (donkey, oil, wine, clothes, money, physical strength, compassion. In our culture he would also make representations to the police about security on the Jericho Road).

The church is involved politically if it does nothing: it is voting for the status quo. All it takes for evil to triumph is that 'good' people do nothing. The villains in Jesus' stories were seldom those who did things they ought not to have done; usually they were people who left undone the things they should have done. The rich man let Lazarus lie unhelped at his gate; the servant made no use of his talent – these received the severest condemnation. The opposite of love is not hate, but indifference.

If 'charity begins at home' then we'll ask: 'What needs exist in our neighbourhood, and what resources do we have to meet them?' Day-care facilities, free food for the hungry, a counselling centre (with fees - if any - related to ability to pay), housing for the homeless/elderly, writing letters to keep elected officials honest – these are some beginnings.

However, charity is not justice. A charitable act is a somewhat spontaneous, temporary, non-controversial response to an accident or tragedy. Conditions of injustice are not accidents. They are never 'acts of God' but acts of men and women with power. To relieve victims of injustice demands that the root causes of injustice be addressed and removed. Charitable acts must not be a substitute for this more controversial and radical activism. Giving a pneumonia sufferer a box of tissues may be of some comfort, but it is irrelevant to the victim's recovery, which depends on other factors.

Such activities force us to ask tough questions. Polarisations will occur; we may find ourselves crusading with the 'ratbag element'; and we'll discover that self-interest and power games exist even in churches!

FINALLY, the evils are ubiquitous, huge and complex. But we must not succumb to immobility: let us do something, and be free to learn through failing, if necessary. Let us repent of our sins of omission before we blame others for their sins of injustice. Then let us get involved. Fighting poverty is war: the violence of poverty kills just as surely as bullets. I am convinced, however, that we must fight this war non-violently. Christ gave his life for others who could not save themselves: let us give our lives for the wretched of the earth. Let us begin with ourselves, and in a world of crying need, adjust our lifestyle accordingly. Let us renounce addictions, especially those involving the desire for immediate gratification. Let us be Christ to others, as Luther put it – serving them, being advocates for them, acting as agents for change. Albert Einstein said: 'The problems of the world cannot be solved with mechanisms, but only by changing the hearts and minds of people and speaking courageously.'

Our next chapter will examine the life of a modern 'saint' - Archbishop Helder Camara - who acted on all this better than anyone I've heard of.

Footnotes

[1] See http://data.worldbank.org/indicator/SN.ITKDEFC.ZS for a 'graphic graph' of under-nourishment throughout the world.
[2] More - https://en.wikipedia.org/wiki/Minamata_disease
[3] The World Health Organisation Framework Convention on Tobacco Control.
[4] http://www.foodbank.org.au/wp-content/uploads/2016/05/Foodbank-Hunger-Report-2016.pdf
[5] https://www.academia.edu/190004/Poverty_and_the_Social_Order
[6] See 'Was Jesus a Christian?' http://jmm.org.au/articles/9664.htm

(An earlier version of these two chapters was included in my first book *Recent Trends Among Evangelicals:* http://www.jmm.org.au/articles/12125.htm et.seq.)

Chapter 7
DOM HELDER CAMARA: a modern saint who seriously followed Jesus

> *Mother Teresa once asked Archbishop Helder Camara how he managed to retain his humility. Camara replied that he imagined himself making a triumphant entry into Jerusalem, not as Jesus but as the donkey who carried him. Years later, Mother Teresa reminded Camara of this conversation, saying that she had adapted his advice to Indian conditions by thinking of herself serving God as an old cow!*

How do the best-put-together people get to be like that?

My top three (male) heroes are Jesus of Nazareth, Dom Helder Camara, and Francis of Assisi, in that order. He's one of three 20th/21st century Catholic Archbishops I admire, each of whom chose slightly different routes in opposing violent regimes. (The other two: Pope Francis, and Archbishop Oscar Romero.)

Dom Helder Camara - Archbishop of Olinda and Recife in Brazil - addressed a packed Melbourne Concert Hall on 15 May 1985. After a rapturous welcome, he stilled the crowd by saying - you guessed it! - 'I'm just Christ's little donkey'. When a baby in the balcony cried he stopped, looked intently towards the sound, and with his tears glistening in the spotlights said: 'We want to make the world safe for you, little one!'

In his playful, down-to-earth, simple way he told us: 'Friends, we have forty times the nuclear potential needed to kill all life – not just human life – on our planet.' 'Let us be Christians not only in name, but by our lives.' 'The perpetrators of violence are sinners, yes, but we're all sinners. Help us Holy Spirit!'

'Vatican 2 insisted that the whole church, not just its hierarchy, are the people of God... So we priests must work not just for the poor, but with the poor... Alone we are weak; together we are a force...›

Many (like Jose Comblin introducing *Into Your Hands Lord*, 1987) say he's the 'only Catholic bishop who has a true audience in the non-Catholic world'.

ooOoo

Dom Helder Camara (1909-1999) was for millions the male counterpart of Mother Teresa: a tireless servant of the poor. (And, yes, Mother Teresa is at the very top of my list of admirable women).

He was born into a poor Fortaleza family (his parents had thirteen children, but five of them died very young in a whooping cough epidemic). Ordained a priest in 1931, until 1947/8 he was an educator. But his appointment as auxiliary bishop (1952) and archbishop (1955) of the diocese of Rio de Janeiro led to his developing a high profile – with weekly TV and daily radio programs. He denounced the city's social and racial divisions. With the help of Presidents Juscelino Kubitschek (1956-1961) and Joao Goulart (1961-1964), he initiated many programs to help the poor, acquiring an international reputation as the 'bishop of the favelas' – and making many powerful enemies, not least of which was the US government: a socially progressive Latin America did not fit with US policy in the wake of the Cuban Revolution. On 31 March 1964, President Goulart was overthrown in a military coup supported by the US.

The next day Helder Camara arrived in Recife as Archbishop. He said to the diocese: 'I am a north-easterner talking to northeasterners... In imitation of Christ, I have not come to be served, but to serve.' He avoided wearing the bishops' purple sash, and quickly abandoned the pretentious palace for three rooms in the outbuildings of a parish church. He ate at the taxi-drivers' stall across the road and hitched lifts around the city instead of running an official car. He gave away church land to the landless, set up a credit union, took students out of seminaries to form small communities in the parishes, and created a theological institute in which future priests studied alongside laypeople, even receiving lectures from women.

He was one of the few bishops critical of the military's reign of terror. Progressive priests, social activists, trade union leaders, members of Congress, writers and journalists were tortured and/or imprisoned. Accused of being a 'communist subversive', Helder Camara was exiled in his own country; for thirteen years from 1970, the government banned him from public speaking and forbade even the publication of his name in any media. Although under constant threat of assassination, he refused a bodyguard or even a lock on his door.

One night, a frightened family sought Dom Helder. One of theirs had been arrested and was being tortured in the police barracks. The bishop phoned the chief of police: 'This is Dom Helder. You are holding my brother.' The policeman, surprised, stuttered: 'Your brother, Eminence?' 'Yes, despite our different names, we are sons of the same Father.' The chief made all sorts of excuses and ordered the release of the man...

One of Dom Helder's collaborators, Father Henrique Pereira Neto, was barbarously assassinated in Recife, after being tied up, dragged along the ground, shot three times, and hung from a tree... Another priest, Father Tito de Alencar, was given electric shocks, kicks, and blows with a rod. His torturer asked him to open his mouth to 'receive the sacrament of the eucharist'. When he did they inserted an electrified wire... Helder: 'It's absolutely terrible. I go regularly to hospitals or prisons, or the morgue, to collect or identify collaborators who had disappeared – priests or laypeople...'

But internationally, he was a 'star' – receiving over eighty invitations a year (accepting only four or five). 'And I go not to attack Brazil, but injustice everywhere.' Nominated three times for the Nobel Peace Prize, he missed out (once to Henry Kissinger and Le Duc Tho). So the 'People's Peace Prize' was created for him – worth two and a half times as much (which he donated to agricultural projects in his diocese). He was also awarded the *Pacem in Terris* ('Peace on earth') Award (named after a 1963 encyclical letter by Pope John XXIII that urged all people of good will to secure peace among all nations). And many doctorates – often from prestigious universities (Harvard, Louvain, the Sorbonne, etc.). 'It's never for myself: I'm simply the representative of the people *sem vez sem voz*, with no hope and no voice...'

ooOoo

Dom Helder Camara was a prophet, rather than a revolutionary or theologian. Within the body of this frail man, there beat the ardent and joyful heart of a troubadour, who, like Francis of Assisi, blessed all people (and like Francis loved nature: plants as well as animals). He often said, 'In the heart of a priest, there cannot exist a drop of hatred. We share the same Father, we are blood sisters and brothers, in the blood of Jesus Christ.'

He articulated the suffering of the poor, espousing pacifism (rather than 'passivism'):

- 'The seven capital sins of the modern world: racialism, colonialism, war, paternalism, pharisaism, alienation and fear.'
- 'For me, [humans] are not divided into believers and atheists, but between oppressors and oppressed, between those who want to keep this unjust society and those who want to struggle for justice.'
- 'Charity is not justice... Aid is necessary, but not enough. Until... international trade policy [is addressed] the poor countries will continue to get poorer, to enrich the wealthy countries more and more.'
- 'Capitalism which puts profit before people is intrinsically evil. But a radical version of Catholic social policy is as anti-communist – because we are non-violent – as it is anti-capitalist... I never saw Cuba as a solution... Changing orbits isn't really liberation – becoming a satellite of Russia rather than of the U.S.'
- '28% of incomes in Brazil go to 1% of the population; 80% of the cultivated land belongs to 2% of landowners' (1970, UN Commission for Latin America). 'Paul VI was right to say "The earth was given to us all, not just to the rich." In our continent more than two-thirds live in sub-human conditions.'
- 'Read the encyclicals, especially *Populorum Progressio* which encourages the wealthy to stand in solidarity with the poor.›

More people know Dom Helder's most famous quote than anything else about this great man:

> *'When I give to the poor they call me a saint; when I ask "Why are they poor?" they call me a communist!'*

The 1985 Garth Hewitt song says it well:

And Fortaleza, your most famous son
has shown us all the way,
Dom Helder Camara,
he had the right words to say,
He said when you feed the hungry
they'll call you a saint,
but never ask the question why...
Why are they hungry?
They'll call you a communist
for asking the question why.
For they're hungry from our opulence,
and they are homeless from our greed,
as the rich world makes its living
from the poor world on its knees.
And a nation roams the streets tonight,
you can see them everywhere,
One hundred million children
like an army of despair.

ooOoo

'They'll call you a saint'. Will they? My vote would be 'yes'. For example:

- He knew the difference between Pharisees and saints: 'Pharisees are strict with others; saints are rigorous only with themselves... as generous as the goodness of God, boundless as the mercy of God.'
- Saints are prayerful. Dom Helder had made a vow – 'the vow of the clock' – to rise at 2 am every morning to pray and read poetry, then maybe sleep for a couple of hours before rising at 5 am for Mass at 6:00 am. He kept this vigil every night since seminary.

- Saints tend to inhabit simplicity - the other side of complexity. (Dom Helder had a favourite guardian angel, Jose, with whom he conducted entreaties when in trouble – which was often.)
- Saints are willing to 'cleanse the Temple/ speak truth to power'. To a young 'forceful' bishop who told Camara he disagreed with his 'non-Christian humanism' Dom Helder asked, 'What have you read or heard about my view of the world?' 'Nothing.' 'And have you read other works you denounce?' The bishop meekly answered: 'I can see that today is going to be a turning-point in my life!'
- In their friendships, saints include everyone from popes and cardinals (especially Montini and Suenens), to ordinary poor folks.
- Saints know their spiritual gifts and use them. One of Camara's was networking, e.g. his brilliant behind-the-scenes lobbying-for-the-poor at Vatican 2 and his various efforts (e.g. Medellin) at convening conferences of bishops.
- Dom Helder was obedient to his superiors and was a faithful Roman Catholic to the end. 'Yes,' he said, 'I argue [with everyone] but my bishop must always have the last word'.
- Miracles? How about these: those sent to kill this archbishop, disguised as beggars or taxi-drivers, could not bring themselves to do it, but confessed and asked forgiveness from their intended victim.
- Saints are humble (probably helped by his shortness of stature - he was just over five feet tall and weighing about 120 pounds). There's real danger of pride in humility: 'Look at me!' he used to say, cheekily. 'I am a poor bishop, a bishop of the poor! Not like those bourgeois bishops!'. His regular prayer was that of St. Francis: 'Pray to the Lord that I may become what people think I am'...

- He did not claim to be a scholar. 'My education thesis was a disgrace: I haven't kept a single copy of it and I hope no one else ever finds one!'

  He wrote meditations in his vigil-time, perhaps read them to a few friends, then destroyed them. ('Flowers bloom, then must fade...'). Fortunately, some survived, like these (from *A Thousand Reasons for Living*):

  By the grace You grant me
  of silence without loneliness,
  give me the right to plead,
  to clamour
  for my brothers and sisters
  imprisoned in
  a loneliness without silence!

  ~~~

  It is worth any sacrifice,
  however great or costly,
  to see eyes that were listless
  light up again,
  to see someone smile
  who seemed to have forgotten
  how to smile;
  to see trust reborn
  in someone
  who no longer believed
  in anything
  or Anyone. [1]

ooOoo

I once invited Dom Helder to write a chapter for a book (with a 'discursive meditation' flavour) I was editing. His postcard reply (in Portuguese):

'If the Lord gives I will give…
Shalom! Dom Helder.'

How can you argue with that? I've used this response ever since when asked to do something beyond my wisdom or outside my time constraints!

Footnote

[1] *A Thousand Reasons for Living*, (Fortress Press, 1981) pp. 63, 112.

Chapter 8
PHARISEES ANCIENT AND MODERN

> *Here we try to make sense of Dom Helder Camara's inclusion of 'Pharisaism' in his list of modern evils...*

Being an itinerant ('hit-run') preacher has some advantages. I remember a Sunday evening service in a conservative church in rural Victoria, Australia. They had big black Bibles and severe expressions... And they knew their Bibles, and were proud of that.

It was a smallish group, so I decided to engage them in dialogue:

'Who knows who the Pharisees were?' They did. 'The Pharisees got a pretty nasty press in the New Testament – particularly Matthew.'

'Now tell me all the good things you can think of about the Pharisees.'

I wrote them up on a blackboard:

The Pharisees knew their Bibles; were disciplined in prayer; fasted twice a week; gave about a third of their income to their church; were moral (very moral); many had been martyred for their faith; they attended 'church' regularly; they were evangelical/orthodox; and evangelistic (Jesus said they'd even cross the ocean – a fearful thing for Jews – to win a convert)...

There was a deep silence.

I asked 'Peter' sitting at the front: 'What's wrong?' He pointed to the list and said 'That's us!' 'Is it?" I responded. 'Then you've got a problem: Jesus said these sorts of people are children of the devil!'

Then we did an inductive exercise on the question: 'What's so wrong with this list of admirable qualities?' Short answer:

it omits what was most important for Jesus. Whenever in the Gospels he used a prefatory statement like 'This is the greatest/ most important thing of all...' none of the above was emphasised by him.

So what were Jesus' emphases? Yes, loving God, loving others, seeking first the kingdom = obeying God the King ... And, from two Gospel verses the evangelicals/orthodox have rarely noticed – Matthew 23:23, Luke 11:42 – justice/love, mercy, faith.

None of these was on the Pharisees' list. But they're the most important of all, according to Jesus.

> *Have you noticed items like justice/love don't get into the classical Christian creeds or confessions of faith or - often, until sometimes recently - 'doctrinal statements' either? (I've written a book about that: Recent Trends Among Evangelicals). [1]*

Back to the Pharisees. Our text (Matthew 12:1-21) is about the problem of religious 'scrupulosity'... Jesus and his disciples were walking on the Sabbath through the fields on their way to the synagogue, to church, and they were hungry. So as the law (Deuteronomy 23:25) allowed, they plucked some ears of corn to eat. But the Pharisees had problems with their 'reaping' on the sabbath. In fact, the disciples were breaking four of the Pharisees' thirty-nine rules about work on the sabbath: technically they were reaping, winnowing, threshing, and preparing a meal!

Now the modern picture of the Pharisees almost certainly trivialises – or demonises – their piety. These were good people with good motives. But they were 'good people in the worst sense of the word'. More of that later...

Jesus' response is to argue from two precedents (lawyers/legalists are at home there) – precedents about necessity and service. David and his friends were hungry, so ate the forbidden bread. [2] Then the priests did a lot of 'work' on the sabbath – killing and sacrificing animals: so Jesus is saying that if sabbath-work has to do with the necessities of life and duties of sacred service, it's O.K. and the 'spirit' of the fourth commandment is not violated. Then Jesus reinforces all this with three arguments: someone greater than the temple is here; God wants mercy to have priority over sacrifice; and 'the Son of man is Lord of the sabbath'. Or, as the *New Interpreters' Bible Commentary* puts it (in a way that would appeal to a rabbinical way of arguing): 'Since the priests sacrifice according to the law on the sabbath, sacrifice is greater than the sabbath. But mercy is greater than sacrifice... so mercy is greater than the sabbath' [3] I like Eugene Peterson's translation of this section in *The Message:* 'There is far more at stake than religion. If you had any idea what this Scripture meant – "I prefer a flexible heart to an inflexible ritual" – you wouldn't be nit-picking like this.' [4]

Then we have the story of the man with the withered hand. Jerome, the fourth century bishop-scholar, says some ancient Gospels tell us his name was Caementarius – a bricklayer – and he said to Jesus: 'Please heal my hand so that I can earn a living by bricklaying rather than begging'. The Pharisees challenge him: 'Is it lawful to heal on the sabbath?' Now there's a technicality behind that question, and Jewish scribes used to debate it: is it lawful for a physician to heal on the sabbath? If the answer is 'yes', how about someone else, like a prophet? The Shammaite Pharisees did not allow praying for the sick on the sabbath, but the followers of Hillel allowed it. Arguments, arguments: 'arguments by extension' to which Jesus answers with an 'argument by analogy'. If the sabbath laws allow you to help a sheep, why not a person? (But then, the Essenes wouldn't have rescued a sheep either: gets complicated!).

So Jesus healed the man. Two notes at this point:

1. Jesus asked the man to stretch out his hand, to do as much as he could. Jesus often did that in his healings. It's the same today: we get help any way we can, and do what we can. Jesus still heals: sometimes slowly (always slowly in cases of sexual/emotional abuse), sometimes instantly; sometimes with, sometimes without, the help of medicine...

2. I was a co-speaker at a conference with the Korean, Dr Paul Yonggi Cho, pastor of the largest church in the world. He said: 'Every miracle recorded in the New Testament, including the raising of the dead, has also happened in Korea: we are praying for some miracles not mentioned in the Bible, nor recorded in Christian history. Like the replacement of a limb – an arm or a leg – that's not there. We're "believing God" for miracles like that.'

Back to the Sabbath: what's it all about? Two things, basically: faith and rest. Faith that God will supply our needs if we don't have to work all the time; and rest so that our lives will be in balance. As you may know, I counsel clergy: that's what John Mark Ministries is about. They're often burned out. But when they are, it's almost always associated with a failure to take the idea and practice of sabbath seriously. They don't take a day off: a day off is any day (for pastors it's often Thursday, with the upcoming Sunday's preparation all done!) when from getting up to going to bed at night you are not preoccupied with your vocation.

Isn't it interesting that in our leisure-oriented culture, there's also more fatigue? A lot of people are just plain tired. The five-day work week is a recent innovation, but 'leisure' and 'sabbath-rest' are not the same.

In his excellent book *Ordering Your Private World*, Gordon McDonald has a chapter 'Rest Beyond Leisure' which I urge you to read. He writes: 'God was the first "rester"... Does God need to rest? Of course not. But did God choose to rest? Yes. Why? Because God subjected creation to a rhythm of rest and work that he revealed by observing the rhythm himself, as a precedent for everyone else... [For us] this rest is a time of looking backward. We gaze upon our work and ask questions like: "What does my work mean? For whom did I do all this work? How well was my work done? Why did I do all this? What results did I expect, and what did I receive?" To put it another way, the rest God instituted was meant first and foremost to cause us to interpret our work, to press meaning into it, to make sure we know to whom it is properly dedicated'. [5]

The Pharisees had lost sight of the essence of the sabbath. Alister McGrath says in his NIV Bible Commentary: 'The Sabbath was instituted to give people refreshment, rather than to add to their burdens'. [6] Precisely how you keep the Sabbath today will be governed by love for God and neighbour, and the kind of work you do. If you're a manual worker, rest. If you're sedentary, do something physical. Make sure it's 'recreational' for you – re-creating your body, mind, emotions and spirit.

Sometimes I talk to a pastor who is being 'destroyed' by Pharisees. They are still with us. Why? It's all about what American social scientists call 'mindsets': the mindset of the Pharisee and that of the prophet are antithetical: they can't get along. Let me explain.

The Pharisee is concerned about law: how to do right. Now there's nothing wrong with that as it stands. Except for one thing:

you can keep the law and in the process destroy persons. I have a friend who lectured in law in one of our universities, before he got out of it all in disgust. He said with some conviction: 'The whole of our Western legal system is sick, unjust. For one thing: if you're rich, and can afford the cleverest advocacy, you have a pretty good chance of not going to jail; but not if you're poor.' There's something wrong with a system supposed to preserve 'fairness' when double-standards operate...

There's a tension between law and love. Law is to love as the railway tracks are to the train: the tracks give direction, but all the propulsive power is in the train. Tracks on their own may point somewhere, but they're cold, lifeless things. But love without law is like a train without tracks: plenty of noise and even movement but lacking direction. Both law and love ultimately come from God. We need God's laws to know how to set proper boundaries and behave appropriately: without good laws we humans will destroy one another. Prophets, in the biblical sense, try to tie law and love into each other. The Old Testament prophets were always encouraging the people of God to keep the law of God.

But the greatest commandment is love: love of God and of others.

Footnotes

[1] http://www.jmm.org.au/articles/12125.htm et seq.

[2] Though note that when King Uzziah invaded the sacred area from another motive – pride – he was struck with leprosy (2 Chronicles 26:16).

[3] *New Interpreters' Bible Commentary,* Abingdon, 1995, p. 278.

[4] Eugene Peterson, *The Message.* https://www.biblegateway.com/versions/Message-MSG-Bible/

[5] *Ordering your private world,* Highland, 1985, pp.176-7.

[6] Hodder and Stoughton, 1995, p. 242.

Chapter 9
WHY MOST DO - BUT SOME DON'T - BELIEVE IN THE EXISTENCE OF GOD

> *Request sent by a student to a Christian enquiry agency:*
> *'We are doing God this term; please send me full details and pamphlets...'*

Common exchange in Israel:

'I'm an atheist.'

'Are you a Muslim atheist, a Jewish atheist, or a Christian atheist?'

(Where else on this planet could a conversation like that happen?).

Most believe that God exists? Yes, most in our world, and most throughout history.

Two key background factors:

1. **'God behaving badly'**. C. S. Lewis (in *The Problem of Pain*): 'If God were good, he would wish to make his creatures perfectly happy, and if God were almighty, he would be able to do as he wished. But the creatures are not happy. Therefore God lacks either goodness, or power, or both.' [1]. This idea was behind Lewis' stance that he did not believe that God existed, and was very angry about God not existing. The principal objection thoughtful/sensitive people have about the existence of a good God is the prevalence of awful suffering. [2]

2. **'God-followers behaving badly'**. Churches and their leaders are getting an increasingly bad press for abusing people - and/

or - using the imagery of the Good Samaritan - leaving them on the side of the road. [3]

SO: WHY DO SOME THOUGHTFUL PEOPLE REJECT THE EXISTENCE OF A DEITY? And apparently the number is growing in Western countries... 'Spiritual but not religious' is an increasingly popular response to census religion questions in countries like mine (Australia).

Some scientists, like Richard Dawkins: 'Darwin made it possible to be an intellectually fulfilled atheist'. [4]

Some philosophers... A. J. Ayer: 'There can be no way of proving that the existence of a god... is even probable'. **Peter Singer** makes a strong point about his objection to belief in a good God based on the awful reality of human and animal suffering. [5] Psychoanalysts like **Sigmund Freud:** 'Religion is a mass-delusion that reshaped reality to provide a certainty of happiness and a protection from suffering'.

Sociologists like Emile Durkheim: 'Religion was something produced by human society, and had nothing supernatural about it'.

Political philosophers like **Karl Marx:** 'Belief in a non-existent God has been a tool used by capitalists to keep the working-class under control. It's been 'the opium of the masses'. [6] Sections of the media like this, from BBC online: 'God is perfectly loving. God knows that human beings would be happier if they were aware of the existence of a loving God. So if such a God existed, he would make sure that everyone knew it. There are lots of people who aren't aware of the existence of a loving God. Therefore, such a God does not exist.' [7]

Religious and literary critics like **Christopher Hitchens:** 'Many religions now come before us with ingratiating smirks and outspread hands, like an unctuous merchant in a bazaar.

They offer consolation and solidarity and uplift, competing as they do in a marketplace. But we have a right to remember how barbarically they behaved when they were strong and were making an offer that people could not refuse. [8] [9]

ooOoo

And now: 'WHAT ARE THE BEST REASONS - IN WHAT ORDER - FOR SOMEONE CHOOSING TO BELIEVE IN [THE EXISTENCE OF] GOD?

1. **First a note about 'religion'.** Anglican pastor/scholar Rev. Dr Michael Jensen describes the 'no religion' option in the Australian census as 'a lie.' 'There's no such thing as a non-religious human being… "Religion" names the things to which we are 'bound'… And there is something in the human being that seeks out these bindings in the things that transcend us. John Lennon was simply kidding himself when he asked us to "imagine no religion". The question is not "religion yes or no", but which religion'? [10]

2. **And a note about science:** That the physical universe we know is apparently 14 billion years old tells us nothing about who created it or why. Science and religion are addressing different questions. For example, science cannot help us with 'Why is there something rather than nothing?' 'God is the best explanation why anything exists at all' claims William Lane Craig, an Evangelical apologist. Scientists employ 'instrumental reason', theists 'radical reason', which is open to transcendent reality.

3. **It is too simplistic** to talk in terms of being 'hard-wired' or 'programmed' to believe in God. Environmental factors apply: humans are not naturally monotheistic. The supernatural

instinct could express itself in polytheism, pantheism, or other belief systems. [11]

4. **For the moment** we'll leave a discussion about the greater integrity of an agnostic rather than an atheistic stance for 'Divine Phenomena' which are 'beyond our ken'. [12]

ooOoo

MY JOURNEY: Here are my notes on the various classical routes from non-theism to theism/Christianity. I've put them in the order I've experienced them (both in terms of time, and relevance).

- My main reason for (a) believing in the existence of God and (b) defining my understanding of that God in a particular way? Simple: I believe in the existence of God - and have a view about what kind of God we are talking about - because I am committed to Jesus. Now all the questions about the historicity of the events recorded in the four Gospels - Matthew, Mark, Luke and John - and whether we can agree with the Jesus described there especially when he talks about himself - belong in another chapter. Let me just mention two formative influences in my thinking: (1) I trust the scholarly work of people like the Evangelical theologians Professor F. F. Bruce a generation ago, and (2) the contemporary historian/theologian Bishop N. T. Wright. And (3) popular writers like the lawyer Lee Strobel. (Example: "I'll admit it: I was ambushed by the amount and quality of the evidence that Jesus is the unique Son of God... I shook my head in amazement. I had seen defendants carted off to the death chamber on much less convincing proof! The cumulative facts and data pointed unmistakably towards a conclusion that I wasn't entirely comfortable in reaching.")[13] Even more important than questions of historicity and polemics is the compelling attraction of the person of Jesus. In the words of the 'Jesus Freaks' of half a century ago: *"If God is like Jesus, nothing is too good to be true!"* And God-in-Jesus experienced the horrors of human suffering to the full. The answer to the problem of evil isn't a theory, it's a life.

- MISSION: I am committed to 'following' Jesus, doing in my world in a small way what he did in his: living a lifestyle of 'radical discipleship' in the spirit of the Sermon on the Mount. And to agreeing with Jesus' summary of 'The Key to Knowledge' (Luke 11:52) - Justice and Love (Luke 11:42) - where he endorsed the sentiments expressed by the Hebrew prophets, summarised by Micah's headline (Micah 6:8: Acting justly, loving mercy, walking humbly with our God). [14]
- COMMUNITY: The Church is Jesus' plan - via four 'spiritual' (rather than simply 'religious') activities - to change the world (through worship, community, formation, and mission). In other words, I opt for the 'Bruderhof option' (serving Christ/others in the world), rather than the 'Benedictine option' (retreating from the world). [15] (And all the biblical leaders spent a disproportionate amount of their lives in deserts). [16] [17]
- However, when people summarise their experience of coming to faith, 'most are Christians because they've met one.' And being born into a Christian family/church provides a strong likelihood of one's later adult commitment.
- Then there's the influence of (respected) Christians/theists who we may not have met. For example, in his autobiography *Surprised by Joy* C. S. Lewis says G. K.

Chesterton and George MacDonald deeply influenced his journey towards surrendering to Jesus Christ.

- In terms of philosophical reasoning, some are impressed by arguments which have been around from medieval times - the ontological argument, the argument from design, God as first cause [18].
- 'Evangelical' traditions affirm that Jesus entered our world of flesh and blood, tears and death. He suffered for us. 'Mr Evangelical' John Stott: 'I could never myself believe in God, if it were not for the cross. The only God I believe in is the one Nietzsche ridiculed as "God on the Cross." [19] And I've met several academics for whom the clincher was their conviction that Jesus' resurrection actually happened. New Testament scholars like Gary Habermas, William Lane Craig, and N. T. Wright, have made the case for Christ's resurrection more airtight than ever. Wright's magnum opus, the 700-odd page *The Resurrection of the Son of God*, is the best contemporary book about why Jesus' resurrection is the best explanation for what really happened on that Easter morning. But yes, of course, the Jesus Seminar and other scholars have alternative views, some of which may be summarised 'Resurrections of dead people don't happen, so it didn't happen in this instance.' [20]
- Back to science. Evolutionary theory and science offer marvellous explanations of how; they offer no explanations of why. 'According to Stephen Hawking, a minute increase of about one part in a million million in the density of the universe one second after the Big Bang would have meant a recollapse of the universe after some ten years. A similar decrease in density would have resulted in a largely empty universe after the same time' [21] Then there's the powerful

Christian testimony of scientists who are experts in their field: like Galileo and Kepler (astronomy), Pascal (hydrostatics), Boyle (chemistry), Newton (calculus), Linnaeus (systematic biology), Faraday (electromagnetics), Cuvier (comparative anatomy), Kelvin (thermodynamics), Lister (antiseptic surgery), and Mendel (genetics). [22] I remember when I was a staff worker with the Australian InterVarsity Fellowship being impressed with the fact that there was then a higher proportion of Science than Humanities graduates who were committed Christians.

- In the humanities field, Australian academic and journalist Greg Sheridan. My summary: The philosophers of ancient Greece, long before the birth of Christ, reasoned their way to God. This is most often associated with Aristotle, but it was a movement among many philosophers and poets of ancient Greece. Their insights were integrated into Christianity in the 13th century by the greatest of the Christian philosophers and theologians, Thomas Aquinas. Famously, Thomas provided his five ways to God through reason. Some Christians mistakenly took to referring to them as the five proofs of God. In truth, by reason alone you cannot absolutely prove God or disprove him. Thomas was trying to understand, not to prove, though understanding often leads to belief.

- First, Thomas suggested that motion had to start somewhere, that there had to be an unmoved mover. Second, the chain of cause and effect is so long, but it too had to start somewhere; there had to be an uncaused cause. Third, contingent beings — that is, beings who rely on some antecedent for their existence — must inevitably proceed from a being who relies on nothing for their existence, a necessary being. Fourth, there is so much goodness in the world, it must correspond to or proceed from a self-sufficient goodness. And fifth, the

non-conscious agents in the world behave so purposefully that they imply an intelligent universal principle.
- 'There's Edith Stein, a brilliant 20th century philosopher. As an atheist, Edith was shocked when she discovered the writings of Catholic philosopher, Max Scheler. As one account of her conversion puts it: "Edith was enthralled by Scheler's eloquence in expounding and defending Catholic spiritual ideals. Listening to his lectures on the phenomenology of religion, she became disposed to take religious ideas and attitudes seriously for the first time since her adolescence, when she had lost her faith and given up prayer". Edith Stein would eventually convert to Catholicism and die a martyr. She is now known as St Teresa Benedicta of the Cross.' [23]
- Then, with some there's a yearning for 'God-if-God-exists' which leads to a study of the Christian Scriptures, and a 'prayer of surrender'. Here's a good description of C. S. Lewis' 'journey to faith': At age seventeen, Lewis wrote to long-time friend Arthur Greeves, 'I believe in no religion. There is absolutely no proof for any of them'. But later while riding on a bus in Oxford, Lewis surrendered to God - the most 'dejected and reluctant convert in all England'. Later, Lewis wrote to Arthur, 'Christianity is God expressing himself through... the actual incarnation, crucifixion and resurrection' [of Jesus Christ]. [24]
- Another route some follow towards a Christian commitment involves their own exploration into prayer and the reading of the sacred Scriptures. One example: Author Devin Rose on his blog writes: 'I began praying, saying, "God, you know I do not believe in you, but I am in trouble and need help. If you are real, help me." He started reading the Bible to learn about what Christianity said... Once Rose began to read the Scriptures and talk to God, even as a sceptic, he found himself

overwhelmed by something very real: 'Still, I persevered. I kept reading the Bible, asking my roommate questions about what I was reading, and praying. Then, slowly, and amazingly, my faith grew and it eventually threatened to overwhelm my many doubts and unbelief. And the rest was history for the now rising Catholic apologist and author of *The Protestant's Dilemma.*' [25]

- Exploring the 'Classical Proofs' for God's Existence. Honest philosophers follow the best arguments wherever they may lead. Dr Ed. Feser (*The Road From Atheism*), recounts the shocking effect of opening himself to the arguments for the existence of God: 'As I taught and thought about the arguments for God's existence, and in particular the cosmological argument, I went from thinking "These arguments are no good" to thinking "These arguments are a little better than they are given credit for" and then to "These arguments are actually kind of interesting." Eventually it hit me: "Oh my goodness, these arguments are right after all!"'

- Feser concludes: 'Speaking for myself, anyway, I can say this much. When I was an undergrad, I came across the saying that learning a little philosophy leads you away from God, but learning a lot of philosophy leads you back. As a young man who had learned a little philosophy, I scoffed. But in later years and at least in my own case, I would come to see that it's true.' [26]

- Order in the Universe. Antony Flew was one of the 20th Century's most famous atheists. He debated William Lane Craig and others on the existence of God. But eventually his recognition of the profound order and complexity of the universe, and its apparent fine-tuning, was a decisive reason for the renowned atheist to change his mind about God's existence. In an interview with Dr Ben Wiker, Flew explains:

"[I had a] growing empathy with the insight of Einstein and other noted scientists that there had to be an Intelligence behind the integrated complexity of the physical Universe." He concluded that it was reasonable to believe that the organisation of space, time, matter and energy throughout the universe is far from random. 'The second was my own insight that the integrated complexity of life itself - which is far more complex than the physical Universe - can only be explained in terms of an Intelligent Source. I believe that the origin of life and reproduction simply cannot be explained from a biological standpoint... The difference between life and non-life, it became apparent to me, was ontological and not chemical. The best confirmation of this radical gulf is Richard Dawkins' comical effort to argue in *The God Delusion* that the origin of life can be attributed to a "lucky chance". If that's the best argument you have, then the game is over. No, I did not hear a Voice. It was the evidence itself that led me to this conclusion.' [27]

- Another critical perspective (critical in both senses): 'Can you name any atheistically-inspired charitable organisations or enterprises? And I don't mean non-religious humanitarian ones like UNICEF. I mean ones specifically inspired by atheism. I mean ones founded by prominent atheists like Friedrich Nietzsche, Jean-Jacques Rousseau, Bertrand Russell, Christopher Hitchens, Richard Dawkins and/or Lawrence Krauss... Until I discover the atheistic equivalents of a Mother Teresa, a Desmond Tutu, a William Booth, a William Wilberforce or a Martin Luther King, I will remain of the view than the Christian contribution to the well-being of humankind is unrivalled -- and in particular, certainly unrivalled by that of atheism. [28]

- BEAUTY. The great theologian, Hans Urs von Balthasar, wrote: 'Beauty is the word that shall be our first. Beauty is the last thing which the thinking intellect dares to approach, since only it dances as an uncontained splendour around the double constellation of the true and the good and their inseparable relation to one another.' Father von Balthasar held strongly to the notion that to lead non-believers to belief in God we must begin with the beautiful. Dr Peter Kreeft calls this the Argument from Aesthetic Experience. The Boston College philosopher testifies that he knows of several former atheists who came to a belief in God based on this argument. In classic Kreeftian fashion, he puts forward the argument in the following way: 'There is the music of Johann Sebastian Bach. Therefore there must be a God. You either see this one or you don't.' [29]

ooOoo

Bonaventure spoke of God as one "whose centre is everywhere and whose circumference is nowhere." [30]

I hope that was all not too 'heavy-going'. Your experience? Have all some of these factors featured in your thinking? In what order?

And if you've drifted away from Theism/Christianity, which factors were relevant, in what order?

Again, my view: 'If God is like Jesus, nothing is too good to be true'.

> Now let's study (in the next chapter) the life of the God-follower who seemed to have no doubts at all about God's existence: Billy Graham, who died as these chapters were being written...

Footnotes

[1] C. S. Lewis, *The Problem of Pain* http://www.jmm.org.au/articles/1174.htm

[2] In addition to chapter two on abuse in this book, there's a whole chapter on pain/suffering coming up in a forthcoming volume in this series.

[3] Consider persecuted Rohingyas, the homeless, victims of abuse, LGBTIs, etc.

[4] Richard Dawkins, *The Blind Watchmaker,* 1986, where he suggests that the theory of evolution explains the variety of life forms on earth without any reference to God. He was criticised by some theists as 'a kind of atheist fundamentalist'. See https://en.wikipedia.org/wiki/The_Blind_Watchmaker. It's interesting that a pantheist in the Sufi tradition, Reza Aslan, who has published his book - *God, a Human History* (Bantam Press) - questions the validity of all monotheistic and polytheistic belief systems, but is not a dismissive atheist. He reckons Richard Dawkins is 'a buffoon, embarrassing himself every day'.

[5] The Case for God, *The Melbourne Anglican*, May 2012, p. 5.

[6] http://www.bbc.co.uk/religion/religions/atheism/beliefs/reasons_1.shtml

[7] http://www.bbc.co.uk/religion/religions/atheism/beliefs/reasons_1.shtml

[8] *God is Not Great: How Religion Poisons Everything* by Christopher Hitchens, https://www.goodreads.com/work/quotes/3442838-god-is-not-great-how-religion-poisons-everything

[9] See also https://www.youtube.com/watch?v=dbhFXpI8DHA. Visit for a good summary on the world's 'Top 50 atheists

today.' Good article on today's leading atheists: https://thebestschools.org/features/top-atheists-in-the-world-today/

[10] *My God My God - is it Possible to Believe Anymore?* https://www.spectator.com.au/2016/07/i-dont-believe-in-no-religion/

[11] *Cognition, Religion and Theology Project,* led by Justin Barrett (et al.) from the Centre for Anthropology and Mind, Oxford University

[12] I came across an excellent list of eight factors recently (http://www.wordonfire.org/.../why-atheists-change-their.../4729/)

[13] Lee Strobel, *The Case for Christ*, Zondervan 1998, p. 264.

[14] See other chapters in this book on these topics.

[15] Note: the 'Benedictine option' is not limited to Catholic or Orthodox eremitical retreatants: it is also pervasive in Protestant and sectarian groups, which have often formed quasi-religious clubs which have no - or little - influence in their world. Certainly the Benedictines - and other Orders which sponsor retreats - perform a necessary service for the whole church, and even people with no connection to a church.

[16] Perhaps Facebook and other 'Social Media' are contemporary vehicles of 'mission' which in some respects may influence more people for God/good than any church.

[17] There's a high correlation here between the beliefs of the society we were brought up in, rather than radical conviction... As I learned in a Sociology Master's degree, 'mission' and 'community' can be 'reinforcement factors': being a propagandist and associating with those

of similar views reinforce mutually-held beliefs. So this quest is essentially about 'what I'm on this planet for', rather than simply 'ticking boxes in a belief system'. You can tick boxes but not change anything. The two creatures in the New Testament who were known for 'ticking boxes' were the Pharisees and demons.

[18] https://www.utm.edu/staff/jfieser/class/110/5-medieval.htm

[19] https://www.goodreads.com/quotes/416309-i-could-never-myself-believe-in-god-if-it-were

[20] Visit N. T. Wright's books discussing Jesus with John Dominic Crossan and with Marcus Borg: brilliant summaries of a conservative and liberal view of Jesus and the Resurrection: http://www.jmm.org.au/articles/26020.htm, http://www.jmm.org.au/articles/14576.htm, http://www.jmm.org.au/articles/29700.htm. See also Alister McGrath's book, *Surprised By Meaning* (Westminster John Knox Press, 2013).

[21] Stephen Hawking, *Black Holes and Baby Universes and Other Essays,* Bantam Dell, 1993, p. 130 http://www.jmm.org.au/articles/23980.htm

[22] http://www.wordonfire.org/.../why-atheists-change-their.../4729/

[23] From an excellent article on the Existence of God published in *The Australian* newspaper (October, 2017), (but which is impossible to access beyond the advertisements. https://myaccount.news.com.au/sites/theaustralian/subscribe.html?sourceCode=TAWEB_WRE170_a_GGL&mode=premium&dest=http://www.theaustralian.com.au/news/inquirer/the-god-question-listen-to-your-inner-voice/news-story/2fe03ae045e5540e04e85bb44e665151&memtype=anonymous). This -

even with the bad language - gives you an idea of his approach. http://www.atheistfoundation.org.au/forums/showthread.php?t=30604&page=1

[24] http://www.cslewisinstitute.org/node/48

[25] http://www.wordonfire.org/.../why-atheists-change-their.../4729/

[26] Edward Feser, *The Last Superstition: A Refutation Of The New Atheism*. (St Augustine's Press, 2008). Also see Kevin Vost's *From Atheism to Catholicism: How Scientists and Philosophers Led Me to the Truth*.

[27] For a more in-depth account of Flew's change of mind on God's existence, read *There Is A God: How The World's Most Notorious Atheist Changed His Mind*. (HarperCollins US, 2008)

[28] Rowan Forster in various letters to *The Age* newspaper.

[29] For more from Dr Kreeft, see his *Twenty Arguments For The Existence Of God* (Truthbomb apologetics).

[30] http://myemail.constantcontact.com/Richard-Rohr-s-Meditation--Being-in-God.html?soid=1103098668616&aid=vDUc4fZ9Yzs

Chapter 10
BILLY GRAHAM
Life, ministry and legacy

> *I was physically close to Billy Graham only once. Forty of us gathered in a church leaders' conference, somewhere in middle America (I forget where). He held us spellbound for about half an hour. At the close, the chairman thanked him, then said, 'Let us bow our heads in prayer.' We all obediently did that and closed our eyes. When we opened them again, Billy Graham had vanished! There were disappointed looks on some of my friends' faces: they thought this might be the one opportunity they'll ever have had to shake the great man's hand. But then, who knows what tricks he has to engage in to preserve his sanity!!!*

Billy Graham was the 20th century's most significant Christian evangelist. He received more accolades and possibly more criticism than any other modern Christian leader.

He was heard live by more than 210 million people, in 185 countries and 417 'crusades'* - and by millions more via television and 'Hour of Decision' radio broadcasts. He saw at least 3 million people commit their lives to Christ. In his 1959 visit to Australia, 130,000 people made a commitment to Christ - almost 2% of the Australian population at that time.[1]

Philip Yancey wrote: 'More than any other Christian preacher, he restored a sense of goodness about the Good News'. (But Jesse Jackson reckoned he would have been 'playing golf with the Pharaohs rather than leading the slaves to freedom'.)

Yancey again: 'When he stepped behind a pulpit, whether speaking to a small group at the White House or the Kremlin, or to millions gathered outdoors in Korea or in Central Park, something supernatural happened. All other concerns of life faded away, and he focused like a laser beam on the one sure thing he knew: the gospel of Jesus Christ and its power to change lives.' [2]

Known as 'America's pastor', Billy Graham was the most sought-after confidential 'chaplain' to US presidents from Truman to Obama. [3]

Upon hearing news of Mr Graham's passing, President Trump spoke for millions when he said 'The GREAT Billy Graham is dead. There was nobody like him! He will be missed by Christians and all religions. A very special man.' [4]

ooOoo

William Franklin Graham was born into a Presbyterian family on 7 November 1918. He died aged 99, suffering complications from cancer, pneumonia and other illnesses, on 21 February 2018.

His teenage years were somewhat preoccupied with baseball and girls but he committed his life to Jesus at the age of fifteen during a 1934 revival led by evangelist Mordecai Ham.[5]

After high school, Graham signed on as a Fuller Brush salesman, praying before each house call for a sale. If the opportunity arose, he would 'witness for Christ' to whoever opened the door. Graham was Fuller's top regional salesman. (Professor Gary Bouma: 'The first indicator that he could sell anything. Fuller brushes were a quality product and he shifted his talents to another quality product and became one its most successful salespersons. He made Christianity a marketable brand'.) [6]

His alma maters were first, Bob Jones College, but there he chafed against its puritanism.[7]

He left for Florida Bible Institute - where, in 1937 on a golf course, he cried out: 'All right, Lord! If you want me, you've got me... No girl or anything else will ever come first in my life again. You can have all of me from now on. I'm going to follow you at all cost'.

Then via a scholarship he went to the solidly Evangelical Wheaton College, Chicago, where he met his future wife Ruth Bell (daughter of missionaries to China). They had five children.

He was ordained by a Southern Baptist Church in 1939. In the 1940s, Billy was a dynamic speaker for Youth for Christ, before holding his first mass rally in 1947. [8]

His fame 'took off' after a breakthrough 1949 Los Angeles tent 'crusade' - which had to be extended from three to eight weeks due to the overflow crowds, partly a result of the publicity ordered by publisher William Randolph Hearst ('Puff Graham!') who was impressed with Graham's potent mix of scripture and apocalyptic anti-communism (an approach Graham would later abandon). A string of favourable stories followed in *Time*, *Newsweek* and *Life*.

ooOoo

Billy and Ruth Graham had unique connections with the British royal family and were often invited to share various occasions/receptions with them on both sides of the Atlantic.[9]

Early in her reign, Queen Elizabeth apparently confided some of her questions about Christian faith and forgiveness to the American.[10]

Surprisingly, the British generally warmed to him. His friend

'Mr Evangelical' John Stott's appraisal: 'If I had to choose one word with which to characterise Billy Graham, it would be integrity. There was no dichotomy between what he said and what he was. He practised what he preached... After postponing the close of the Harringay crusade, it went on to last twelve weeks, becoming a remarkable phenomenon... I went almost every night. Twelve thousand people assembled, night after night, and listened attentively to the message. Each night, I asked myself what brought the crowds, since many of our churches were half-empty? The answer, I thought, was that Graham was the first transparently sincere preacher they had ever heard. There was something authentic about that man. As many media people confessed, "We don't agree with him, but we know he is sincere." [11]

ooOoo

Dr Graham authored more than twenty-five bestselling books, including *Peace with God, The Holy Spirit, Hope for Each Day, The Journey, The Reason for My Hope,* and *Where I Am.*

The Billy Graham Evangelistic Association organised the 1966 World Conference on Evangelism in Berlin and the 1974 International Congress on World Evangelization in Lausanne, Switzerland.

His legacy?

1. His message remained the same right through his preaching life. His words: 'I preach the same message everywhere: "God loves you. God is interested in you. Christ died for you, and he rose from the dead. The message is always the same."'

2. Marrying Evangelicalism with Social Concern. In his book *Approaching Hoof Beats* (1985) Graham writes: 'My basic commitment as a Christian has not changed, nor has my view of the Gospel, but I can no longer proclaim the Cross and the Resurrection without proclaiming the whole message of the Kingdom, which is justice for all. 'The Lausanne Conferences encouraged the Evangelical world to incorporate social justice into their theologies. Berlin (1966) saw 'social involvement' as the enemy of 'biblical evangelism'; many in Lausanne (1974) viewed them as complementary; Wheaton (1983) saw social action and political engagement as integral to evangelism. *The Manila Manifesto* (1989) included these two statements: '8. We affirm that we must demonstrate God's love visibly by caring for those who are deprived of justice, dignity, food and shelter. 9. We affirm that the proclamation of God's kingdom of justice and peace demands the denunciation of all injustice and oppression, both personal and structural; we will not shrink from this prophetic witness.'
3. On race: 'Jesus was not a white man. He was not a black man. He came from that part of the world that touches Africa and Asia and Europe... Christ belongs to all people: the whole world.' He refused to preach to segregated audiences: historic in both the U.S. and apartheid South Africa. "Graham reflects the early uneasiness with integration," says Nancy Ammerman, associate professor of the sociology of religion at Emory's Candler School of Theology. "Although he knew it was morally the correct thing to do, I think he would have preferred if all that could have happened quietly. But we know now that Martin Luther King's calling was not Billy Graham's calling. As it turned out, the black church changed the laws and the white church made sure the laws were obeyed once changed."

4. Integrity: 'Don't be in a room alone with a woman other than one's wife'. 'No more "love (financial) offerings"'.
5. A pastoral ministry to US and world leaders. He didn't push special agendas, otherwise he probably would not have had that access.
6. Ecumenism: 'I think that everybody who loves and knows Christ, whether they are conscious of it or not, are members of the Body of Christ.'[12]
7. Do your own survey: there will still be Billy Graham converts - most probably over 60! - in many if not most churches!

ooOoo

Criticisms?

There were many. A representative sample from a Google search:

1. 'His theology generally was simplistic: captive all his life to the slogans of Middle American Evangelicalism.'
2. 'What are we to make of his staunch support for the war in Vietnam, and his pressing for nuclear attacks on the North?'
3. 'He was trapped in those ignorant times in unthinkingly condemning homosexuality.'
4. 'He got "sucked in" by his "good friend" Richard Nixon, who secretly taped their conversations, and shared his bigotry about Jews controlling the media and promoting pornography. Doesn't he understand the holocaust?' 'Probably Billy Graham's most painful experience of being conned by a pathetic, evil man.'
5. 'In terms of race relations, he could have been more proactive: he had a respectful but cautious friendship with Martin Luther

King Jr. but was wary about breaking the law to confront race issues'. 'Re. race: doesn't his Bible say black-skinned people are to be "hewers of wood and drawers of water"?
6. 'He commented favourably about the confederate flag. Although a Southerner, he should have outgrown the painful history of that awful war.'
7. He was a male chauvinist. Over-ruling his future wife's desire to be a missionary in Tibet, he said "I'll do the leading and you do the following". 'If he had transitioned his mantle to his daughter Anne Graham Lotz, American and world Evangelicalism would have been set on a much more positive course and find itself less of a counter-cultural sect that it has become.'
8. 'His approach would not work today: he would be seen as too strident, too negative, too cerebral, too wordy, and too much the showman. Meanwhile the market has radically differentiated so that many modes are needed to communicate and the message needs grounding in a host of ways, experiences and stories - not a hectoring lecturer.'

ooOoo

The song, 'Thank You, Billy Graham' was released in 2005 on Pat Boone's album, *Glory Train: The Lost Sessions.* Now, thirteen years later, we mourn the world's greatest modern day pastor. Let's give Pat Boone the last word: "If there's anyone in my lifetime who deserves honour it is Billy Graham," Boone, 83, said in an interview. "I think he is the most significant figure since the apostles. I didn't know Peter and I didn't know Paul, but I know Billy Graham".

Resources
1. Watch his funeral here: A six-hour live version: https://www.pbs.org/newshour/nation/watch-live-the-rev-billy-grahams-funeral
2. Touching moments: each of the children, and a clip of Billy Graham's preaching (4 minutes) [https://www.youtube.com/watch?v=YkJB9-rfuc4]
3. President Trump at Billy Graham's Lying in Honour [https://www.youtube.com/watch?v=-C2sv_CKaKM&t=95s]
4. Sociologist/Professor Gary Bouma: An excellent interview: http://radio.abc.net.au/programitem/pe7Ld58apD?play=true

* Note the quotes around 'crusade', a term he would later reject, due to its historic Christian associations resulting in the alienation of Muslims, and others.

Finally, in the next chapter, we move to a more nuanced discussion of the 'truth/truths' of Christianity than Billy Graham's as we ask about Ghandi and other religions.

Footnotes

[1] *Australian Evangelical Alliance,* cited in *Eternity,* March 2018, p. 18.

[2] https://www.christianitytoday.com/ct/2018/billy-graham/

[3] https://www.politico.com/magazine/story/2018/02/21/billy-graham-death-richard-nixon-217039

[4] https://billygraham.org/gallery/billy-graham-pastor-to-the-presidents/

[5] http://www.stevewalburn.com/the-third-coming-of-billy-graham/

[6] Professor Gary Bouma, in an email to the author.

[7] http://www.stevewalburn.com/the-third-coming-of-billy-graham/

[8] https://en.wikipedia.org/wiki/List_of_Billy_Graham%27s_crusades

[9] https://billygraham.org/story/billy-graham-and-the-queen/. See also the Netflix series The Crown - https://www.townandcountrymag.com/leisure/arts-and-culture/a14107629/queen-elizabeth-billy-graham-friendship/

[10] https://www.washingtonpost.com/news/acts-of-faith/wp/2018/01/09/fact-checking-the-crown-queen-elizabeths-faith-and-her-close-relationship-with-preacher-billy-graham/utm_term=.845df3728cae

[11] https://www.christianitytoday.com/ct/2018/billy-graham/john-stott-billy-graham-walking-together-to-glory.html

[12] In a 1997 interview with Robert Schuller, quoted in *Wikipedia.*

Chapter 11
IS GANDHI IN HEAVEN? CHRISTIANITY AND OTHER RELIGIONS

> *'Do you Israelites think you're any better than the far-off Cushites?' (Amos 9:7-8, The Message)*
> *Everybody dies in Adam; everybody comes alive in Christ. (1 Corinthians 15:22, The Message)*
> *'God is dead, Marx is dead, and I don't feel too good myself!' (Ionesco)*

In a pluralistic culture, we are more aware of others' beliefs. A missionary in Nigeria visited a young man in the back street of Lagos. On his bedside table were the *Bible*, the *Book of Common Prayer*, the *Koran*, three copies of *Watchtower* (magazine of the Jehovah's Witnesses), a biography of Karl Marx, a book of Yoga exercises, and *How to Stop Worrying and Start Living* by Dale Carnegie.

These days we travel more, TV shows documentaries of foreign cultures, students study abroad, multiculturalism in the West is here to stay...

Intolerance is increasing too. Militant Hindus have a motto 'Save India from Christian imperialism!' Many Moslem countries make it a punishable offense to proselytise. Then there's Lebanon, and Northern Ireland... Religion and politics can be volatile subjects, particularly when they mix.

Something else has happened that has never happened before. People (to paraphrase T. S. Eliot) have left God not for other gods, they say, but for no gods. It is possible both to deny gods and worship gods – gods like rationality, money, power, sport etc. And it will all lead to an age advancing progressively backwards...

Of all the world's religions, Christianity has the greatest number of followers (33%), followed by Islam (18%), Hinduism (13%), and Buddhism (6%).

ooOoo

What is religion? Definitions are legion: 'what we do with our solitariness'; 'how we relate to others'; 'our answer to fear'; 'an ultimate attempt to enlarge and complete one's personality by finding the supreme context in which we rightly belong'. Everyone is religious, in some sense. Although Freud termed religion 'mass neurosis' – religious believers were infantile, unable to break outgrown ties with their parents — Carl Jung said of his patients over thirty-five, 'all have been people whose problem in the last resort was that of finding a religious outlook on life.'

There is an increasing hunger for religious reality. 'Baby-boomers' are not in church as often as their elders, but they claim to be as religious. They read Shirley Maclaine and play around with the New Age movement. In a noisy world, people searching for 'God who is Sound and Silence' as the Maitri Upanishad puts it are going in larger numbers to Buddhist monasteries and Hindu ashrams — places of quiet serenity, simple life-style, meditation, brief talks and questions. More young people are reading the Hindu *Bhagavad Gita*, the Chinese *I Ching,* or do Yoga, transcendental meditation or Zen courses.

ooOoo

Let's ask the hard questions in order: Was Gandhi a Christian? No, as we saw in the movie, Gandhi, although he admired Jesus, he lived and died a Hindu. But the great British missionary E. Stanley Jones said of him: 'He taught me more of the spirit of Christ than anyone in East or West.'

A harder question: Is Gandhi in heaven? Christians offer three broad answers.

1. **Conservative Christians** have their doubts. The principle of Karma (cause and effect – paying off your own guilt) is poles apart from grace (God's free forgiveness, which you don't deserve). Augustine's theology inspired western Christians to believe that those outside the church are dammed. A more refined view might be Karl Barth's 'Religion is unbelief', or Hendrik Kraemer's conviction that non-Christian religions were not means of salvation in any sense. However, others would argue, what kind of God would organise for most of his human creatures to burn in hell forever - many of them because, by accident of birth, or the disobedience of the Christian minority to evangelize, they had never heard the gospel? Is he not the Father of Jesus, who prayed for those who crucified him? Does he not want all to be saved and come to know the truth (1 Timothy 2:3, 4)?

2. **More liberal Christians** would answer: 'Be tolerant. There's value in all religions. They all lead ultimately to God. Of course, Gandhi is with him!' The problem with this view is its failure to take seriously the question of truth. If the original Christians were 'liberal' there would have been no mission, no universal Church.

3. **Is there a way between** these two extremes? Yes, the more cautious say - 'Only God knows: our eternal destiny is in his hands alone'. With evangelicals like Howard Guinness (*The*

Seekers) or J. N. D. Anderson (*Christianity and Comparative Religion*) they ask: Does God 'accept' only people within the 'covenant community' - whether Jewish (in the Old Testament) or Christian (in the New Testament)? No: what about Melchizedek, Rahab, and Cornelius? Certainly, Jesus Christ is unique; he alone is the Son of God made man. We are not to take everyone's views, mix them up, and get an identikit picture of God. Jesus is the only way to God. But that may not mean that only Christians are saved (see Romans 2:11-16).

At the Second Vatican Council, Roman Catholics moved from *extra ecclesiam nulla salus* (outside the Church, no salvation) to 'The Catholic Church rejects nothing of what is true and holy in other religions'. Devotees of non-Christian religions may be 'implicit believers' or, in Karl Rahner's phrase, 'anonymous Christians'. Hans Kung says these religions may provide ordinary, whereas the Christian Gospel provides extraordinary means of salvation.

Don Richardson (*Eternity in Their Hearts*) says God has revealed himself to more people than we might imagine. The one invisible God is resident in many folk religions. Christianity doesn't replace this revelation, he says, but completes it. Pachacuti, King of the Incas, led a religious reform in the 1400s, encouraging his people to worship Viracocha, the Creator, rather than Inti, the sun god. His hymns to Viracocha sound like the Hebrew Psalms.

When missionaries came to the Santals in India in the 1800s, they found a tradition about Thakur Jiu, 'the Genuine God'. Many became Christians. The Chinese had Shang Ti, the Lord of heaven. The Karens of Burma believed in Y'wa, the true God.

Non-Christian religions are a testimony to people's search for

God. They may be far from the God of Jesus, but God is not far from any one of them. God cares for all his human creatures with a love we who are biased in favour of those who are like us can't imagine. His rain falls on the just and the unjust...

All religions have good and evil elements. As novelist Mary McCarthy observed: religion makes good people good and bad people bad. Christians have burnt heretics, Jews robbed Palestinians of lands and homes, some Hindus still burn widows (sati), tribal witchdoctors put curses on people, Moslems wage religious wars.

(An eminent Egyptian scholar said privately to Hendrik Kraemer: 'I no longer believe in Islam but, if anyone were to attack the prophet publicly, I would kill him!').

Never forget that Jesus was rejected and sent to his death by people who belonged to a highly moral and spiritual religion. But, you say, well, Christianity has sanctioned evil, but in essence it is good. True: people from other religions say the same of their faiths too.

Christianity, said Karl Barth, stands as much under the judgment of the Gospel as other religions. Roman Catholicism will be judged for the Inquisition; and the Protestant John Calvin for standing by as Geneva burned the 'heretic' Servetus...

ooOoo

Will everyone be saved? George Macdonald says all answers to such a question are deceptive. Two things are certain: all who are saved are saved through Jesus Christ. And a merciful God can handle the judgment of his loved creatures without our help! Jesus said everyone will be surprised at the last judgment. We should aim to be secure in our own faith and be open-minded about matters that are God's prerogative.

So why evangelise? To get them into heaven? Yes, but there are better motives: the glory of God, obedience to Christ, and sincere love for others. Although Christ is not known everywhere, he is everywhere. We are called to make him known, not to make him present.

Some don'ts and do's in evangelism: Don't major on the faults in other religions: the faults in your own are bad enough. Don't argue: you may win the argument but lose the person: today the world is a conference table not a lecture hall, so learn to listen as well as you talk. Above all, be compassionate: Jesus preached judgment on Jerusalem when it rejected him, but he also wept for the city. Share your faith, as a beggar sharing bread with another beggar. Ask 'what are my friend's felt needs?' and start there. (An African proverb says 'Hungry people have no ears!').

Invite overseas students home: perhaps your family could 'adopt' one. (Most in the Book of Acts were converted while away from home). Teach English to someone. Encourage your church to translate the service into another language or host an ethnic church.

And, beyond all that, **remember Jesus' approach to Nicodemus.** This cultured man wanted to talk about the contrasts between Jesus' teaching and that of more traditional Judaism. The conversation started courteously enough, but very soon Jesus said to him 'You must be born again!' That is still the essence of the good news – even for the very religious.

ooOoo

Good teaching is found everywhere. In every religion there is something good, but good teaching alone cannot give life.

Life is only to be had through the giver of life, not through the pages of books.[1]

Where is the truth in other faiths? There are three bad ways to solve this problem. One is to lump all religions together and dismiss them all. As G. K. Chesterton once observed, to stop believing in God does not mean that people will believe in nothing. They may substitute a nationalistic for a religious faith, and be more fanatical than before. Another is to affirm that each religion is part of a whole. 'There is only one religion, though there are a hundred versions of it.' (George Bernard Shaw). The third is to be absolutist: only people like me have the truth! Amos (9:7-9) thundered against the exclusivism that believed God only cares for people 'like us'. 'People of Israel, I think as much of the people of Sudan as I do of you...' [2]

God comes to us in Jesus who is the way. We are like people who have fallen into a pit and in that fall have been injured. Our legs and our arms are broken. For anyone to lower a ladder into the pit and say, 'This is the only way out, climb it,' only adds to our desperation. But if the ladder is lowered not for us to climb out, but for one to climb down and lift our broken body into his arms, carrying us upwards and to safety — that is good news indeed! [3]

The neutral observer... looks at the plurality of religions from the outside: for him or her, the existence of more than one true religion is self-evident... The committed believer looks... from the inside...: what is the true religion for me?

I confess openly that my standpoint is that of a Christian. I am convinced that Christianity is the true religion. I cannot prove it — faith can never be demonstrated — but I can offer good reasons, which convince me... We come to a third and ultimate perspective....: there is a vertical dimension, that of the Absolute.

As Christians, we do not believe in Christianity but in God. Christianity, as a complex of dogmatic teachings, liturgical rites and codes of behaviour, does not escape the ambivalence of our human, historical condition. As Karl Barth used to say, religion is always a shaky and relative thing: not religion as such, but the absolute Being to which it is directed is the true absolute. This is the primordial and ultimate reality which we call God, which the Arabs call Allah, which Jews and Indians decline to name, but worship none the less. In relation to this ultimate and absolute reality of God, even the true religion is relative... Even Christianity is *in via:* ours is a Church on pilgrimage, on the way, which has not yet arrived at the goal of seeing God face to face. To admit this is neither liberalism nor relativism nor syncretism; it is faith, pure and simple. [4]

In the past, we have sometimes been guilty of adopting towards adherents of other faiths attitudes of ignorance, arrogance, disrespect and even hostility. We repent of this. Nevertheless, we are determined to bear a positive and uncompromising witness to the uniqueness of our Lord, in his life, death and resurrection, in all aspects of our evangelistic work including interfaith dialogue. [5]

ooOoo

Krister Stendahl is fond of saying that no interfaith conversation is genuinely ecumenical unless the quality of mutual sharing and receptivity is such that each party makes him- or herself vulnerable to conversion to the other's truth. [6]

The other religions are not to be understood and measured by their proximity to or remoteness from Christianity. They are not beginnings which are completed in the Gospel... To fit them into this model is to lose any possibility of understanding them. Moreover, what do the concepts of 'near' and 'far' mean in relation to the crucified and risen Jesus? Is the devout Pharisee nearer or further than the semi-pagan prostitute? Is the passionate Marxist nearer or further than the Hindu mystic? ...Is the Gospel the culmination of religion or is it the end of religion? [7]

> *It has become customary to classify views on the relation of Christianity to the world religions as either pluralist, exclusivist, or inclusivist... [My] position is exclusivist in the sense that it affirms the unique truth of the revelation in Jesus Christ, but it is not exclusivist in the sense of denying the possibility of the salvation of the non-Christian. It is inclusivist in the sense that it refuses to limit the saving grace of God.*

Footnotes

[1] Sadhu Sundar Singh, [Alys Goodwin, *Sadhu Sundar Singh in Switzerland,* Madras: Christian Literature Society, 1989, p. 49.]

[2] Rowland Croucher, from an unpublished sermon, 'Do Other Religions Also Lead to God?'

[3] Henk Booy, quoted by A. M. Watts, *'Christian Claims in a Pluralist Society'* (Christian Century, 106)

[4] Hans Kung, *'Ecumenism and truth: the wider dialogue'* https://lifeinmessiah.org/resources/hidden-christ/

[5] *The Manila Manifesto,* Lausanne Movement, 1989

[6] Leonard Swidler, *'Interreligious and Interideological* Dialogue http://dialogueinstitute.org/dialogue-principles/

[7] Lesslie Newbigin, *The Finality of Christ* (London: SCM Press, 1969)

EPILOGUE
DEALING WITH GRIEF

Dear friends,
The very sad backdrop to this book is the passing away of my wife of nearly fifty-eight years from cancer, on 1 August 2017.

ooOoo

> *A friend, Nils von Kalm, wrote the following article for one of Australia's leading religious journals,* The Melbourne Anglican

Many readers will be aware that Jan Croucher, wife of counsellor and pastor to many, Rowland, has passed away after fighting cancer for the past four years...

Rowland shared on Facebook six weeks before she died (posted June 19, 2017) the depth of grief he experienced as he watched his life partner of more than 50 years become weaker and sleep for most of the day.

His own summary expresses it best:

"Friends, it's taken nearly 80 years to discover my greatest area of ignorance: I have never experienced such deep sadness ever before...

I need your help.

Jan is dozing in the recliner chair next to me. She now sleeps about 22 hours in every day. (At this point she stirred and huskily said 'I'm so weary...').

There's an ache deep in my being... Maybe sooner rather than later I'm going to lose her, the love of my life...

What spiritual/emotional resources are there to cope with the huge void she'll leave in my heart???

As a pastor I've shared 'grief', genuine grief, with hundreds of people.

But this is different. Instead of going away the sadness goes deeper, and deeper..."

ooOoo

The fact that Rowland's post was acknowledged by 520 people and received 253 comments reflects not just the esteem in which he and Jan are held by so many, but that grief touches something inside all of us that goes to the very core of who we are.

Life is difficult. Such were the opening words of M. Scott Peck in his bestseller, *The Road Less Travelled.* In those three words he spelled out what we all know to be true. Death is a constant in this world and is a reality that not one of us will escape unless Jesus returns beforehand.

Viktor Frankl, in his book, *Man's Search for Meaning,* in which he describes his experience as a prisoner in Auschwitz in the Second World War, quotes Friedrich Nietzsche in saying that "To live is to suffer. To survive is to find meaning in the suffering."

When I spoke at a church gathering a few years ago, I told of my own recent suffering. At the time I was going through a divorce and had recently been made redundant from the best job I ever had.

As I spoke to what was a group of mainly young adults, I reminded them that if they haven't experienced intense suffering in their lives yet, they would. It is a rare person who goes through life untouched by suffering that shatters the very foundations of your identity.

What do you do with suffering so intense as that caused by the passing or imminent passing of a life partner of 57 years, or a divorce, or a job loss? We cope in different ways of course. Many seek to escape, unable to face the pain; others try to face the pain alone, isolating themselves, whereas others seek the comfort of loved ones.

I have done all three during my suffering, and I have found that it was only through facing the pain with a few people walking with me, hearing me, that gave me the strength to continue. I emphasise the word 'hearing'. It is so different to just hearing words. As I cried over my divorce and shared my deepest pain with my counsellor, I felt heard. He didn't say a lot, which frustrated me at first (I just wanted him to fix me), but he always affirmed me in my pain, in my shame and in my tears. In the process something shifted in the core of my being. Shame became dislodged and healing began.

Another type of response is that by Horatio Spafford, writer of the hymn, *It Is Well With My Soul*. Spafford wrote that hymn during his own grief. Having lost all four of his daughters in a shipwreck, and in which his wife was the family's only survivor, he embarked on the next ship to be with his wife. When he got to the place where his daughters' ship had gone down, he told the captain to stop the vessel as Spafford went down below and wrote the words to this famous hymn.

As I reflect on Spafford's response, I also think of Job's 'comforters', his friends who told him that he must have sinned in some way to bring his immense suffering on himself. Often the best form of comfort to someone who is in deep suffering is to just sit with them, not say much, and just spend time with them. We crave relationship and comfort in our sadness; we are designed for it, and to just feel heard and acknowledged by a trusted friend works wonders.

The human cry is for love and affirmation. That is what I experienced during my own grief process, and it is what I saw in the hundreds of comments for Rowland when he so courageously expressed his own sadness on Facebook. I have never experienced the death of a life partner, but divorce is a death too, as anyone who has gone through it knows only too well. When you go through such pain, you are stripped bare, and you start to wonder if there will ever be an end to the suffering.

When we acknowledge the pain, we come face to face with our own human fragility. So when the tears well up, it is crucial that we let them flow. At the height of my grief, the pain was so close to the surface that I was able to set aside time in the morning before work to just lie on my bed and sob, and do the same in the evening when I got home. It was like I was able to just turn the tears on and off. It was soul-crushingly painful, but it helped me heal during those long days. Surgery and the subsequent recovery are always painful, but we don't heal unless we go through it.

Life is about how you deal with loss, ultimately to the loss of your life. When you experience deep loss, the pain never actually goes away. It becomes part of you. It may lessen over years but it is always there.

Good psychologists, and good science, tell us that expressing our grief is crucial for healing. This is often more socially acceptable for women than men, and explains the anger and pain that is so pent up in so many men in our culture, and that results in violence to others and to ourselves.

It is just so important for us to cry our tears, to let them flow. There is no timeline for grief. Don't let anyone tell you that you should be over something by now. Such a response, though probably sincere, is dangerous and harmful.

Some of the responses to Rowland's request for wisdom in his post simply suggested that there are no words but tears. I can imagine that he would have felt held in the many arms of love as he read those moving and heartfelt comments.

One of the stages of grief is acceptance. That can sound coldly clinical when you are in the midst of it, but we spend so long trying to deny the pain. The human heart can only bear so much. Our souls ache and our hearts break as we eventually come to realise that what we had before really is gone and is not coming back. It is then that the sobbing, welling up from deep within us, seems to have no end.

I have found that the people I have met who are the most mature, and who 'get it' when it comes to comforting others in their grief, are those who have experienced deep suffering themselves. They are the wounded healers, to use a term by Henri Nouwen. They don't have pat answers or tell you to have more faith; they are the ones who have been through hell and have come out the other side, knowing God more deeply and understanding the Man of Sorrows in a way that few others do. I have always been encouraged that the shortest verse in the Bible, John 11:35, is also the most human, and it was expressed by the Son of God himself.

We have a God who weeps when we weep, who suffers with us, who has been through it all and come out the other side, resurrected but with nail-scarred hands, with a new body but with the wound still in his side. This is the hope for all who suffer. Our wounds forever shape us, but they don't define us. When we think there is no end to grief, we are comforted with the truth that there is also no end to hope.

Jan is with her Lord. Her pain has gone and she awaits resurrection. Her own scars will have shaped her but not defined her, and she finally knows, in the fullest sense of the word, that there are no more tears, no more pain and no more death. And on that wonderful day of resurrection, Rowland will see the love-of-his-life again. I can picture them laughing and embracing together. May that day come soon, because until then we grieve

ooOoo

Here are some of the 255 comments from Rowland's Facebook friends, abbreviated a little. (They may provide some appropriate words and thoughts for your expressions of loving care for grieving friends).

* *Your beautiful sharing of this the most difficult experience of your life is very special and all of us are walking with you... Peace that is beyond our understanding, beyond our hopes, our dreams, our hearts, carry you over the journey ahead...*
* *I have no words. But we have both prayed for you and will again this evening...*
* *I've never met you Rowland. I will be praying for you...*
* *Let the tears flow Rowland, as long and as often as they will... and we will be weeping with you...*
* *Love and prayers to you and Jan. You have so much love in this life, and much more awaits in the next...*
* *All words seem like platitudes... I simply sang 'When peace like a river...' sang it right through, for you...*
* *Some of Parker Palmer's writings from his deep depression are power-filling. And there's whatsyourgrief.com. You are never alone on this journey Rowland... Peace, love, hope, comfort - and rest. These and more we send your way <3*
* *We offer love and prayer, in full measure...*

* *Your community will tend the deep wounds of your loss, Rowland...*
* *Allow others to have faith that God will sustain you Rowland...*
* *Joni Eareckson said in her first book,*
  'Gaze on Jesus and glance at your problems'...
* *Take your time, don't expect anything of yourself, be gentle with yourself... and thank you for sharing your inner feelings with us: I am honoured to thank you...*
* *I lost four loved ones during the past four years... I feel for you Rowland and I trust your faith and hope will sustain you through the days, weeks and months ahead...*
* *My experience of grief is different; there is no single answer; God bless you both at this difficult time...*
* *The caterpillar sheds its skin to reveal the butterfly within... May you find peace and solace in the life you have had together...*
* *God knows and feels your pain: he has you both in his hands...*
* *We are so blessed to have you as our pastor, Rowland...*
* *We cry and pray with and for you...*
* *In my grief, in the midst of pain, holding on to their memories has kept me going. Touching music. A walk through the garden...*
* *I've thought a lot about the fact that it seems so cruel that those with the deepest love then must endure the deepest grief. Be kind to your poor aching heart...*
* *Sorry you are experiencing this sad sad loss...*
* *Express it all - the rage and despair and love and grief... Self-indulgence is permitted - even recommended...*
* *Understand deep in your spirit that those in Christ never*

die. You will see her again. Meanwhile it will be tough, real tough, but you are not alone...
* Pastor, you are so, so deeply loved...
* Praying for strength, comfort and peace...
* Praying for you and your beautiful family...
* What an honour to be a witness to the beauty, love and deep grief you display and feel as you journey through these difficult days...
* Rowland, nothing to say except to know you are deeply loved by many...
* Underneath are the everlasting arms holding you and Jan...
* No words can express the journey of the heart at these times, but it is not the end...
* Writing this has helped me: https://www.periecho.com/single-post/2016/10/16/The-Paradox-of-Transformational-Pain
* We cannot take away the joy or pain but rejoice with you both the true happiness, companionship, joy and partnership the two of you were so blessed to share together...
* Give yourself permission and space to wail, lament, scream and feel (as C S Lewis described it in A Grief Observed). With time the hurt gets less painful...
* Jesus, who said "I am the Alpha and Omega, the first and the last" is with you both right now... and forever..
* You taught me so much, and here in your hour of great need, still teaching us how to approach life... My love to you both...
* Your pain while unique is shared by many...
* Life is a walk with God... each day you return home. Until one day comes and you hear "we are closer to my home than yours: why not keep walking with me..."
* Rowland, all I can say brother, is that you are profoundly

inspirational to us all. God continue to bless, fill and comfort you...

* Jesus walks and weeps through the grief with us, and doesn't judge or condemn, regardless of how much we express our hurt and pain... In time the happy memories outweigh the sadness and the beauty remains. Love to you both...
* Thank you for your open honesty. It has been said, the greater the love the more the pain. So many psalms cry out to the God who loves. Prayer continues for you both...
* 1 Corinthians 13:12: "For now we see through a glass darkly, but then face to face; now I know in part, but then I shall know even as also I am known"...
* I pray that you find souls that have known this grief and have a desire to sit with you...
* Be yourself. Absorb God's love. Give Jan to your Creator because he gave her to you... Thanks for blessing us on Facebook and elsewhere...
* Share your vulnerabilities and also the positives, so that on the darker days you can remember those positives...
* I have no clever words or trite sayings; I pray for you both and ask God to give you peace...
* Oh Rowland - such deep and profound sadness and grief. Know that you have an army of people praying for you at the hour of your and Jan's greatest need. You and Jan will be carried and supported along this next journey as you have been throughout your lives together. God bless you both my dear friends xxx
* Your faith is strong, your love for Jan will see you through. God bless you and sustain you
* May the peace that passes all understanding, guard and protect your dear dear heart and mind in Christ Jesus. The

Man of Sorrows holds you so very close even now...

Ad astra per alas fideles
'To the stars on the wings of the faithful ones.'

ooOoo

And now, a final benediction from me to you all.
'May the good Lord give you all love, faith - and hope.'
Rowland Croucher,
(25/12/2017: *My first Christmas without Jan in sixty years*)

POSTSCRIPT
COMING UP IN FUTURE VOLUMES

The aim of this series of Questions & Responses, is to address the 50 (or more!) 'ultimate issues' which provide conversations between my fellow Christian pastors, and their clienteles.

Feel free to email me (rcroucher@gmail.com) if you have any other suggestions. (Perhaps add a true-to-life story with your nominated topics.)

This first volume addressed a number of core issues - but the remaining collections include some equally tough subjects (and some biographical summaries of special people).

After-life

Ageing, and retirement

Ambiguity

Ananias & Sapphira (people who dropped dead in church)

Atheism (again)

Atonement

Belief-systems and creeds

Bible

Books (my list of must-read-at-least-once-in-your-life-time titles)

Brethren (with a special reference to two people who've experienced them - Garrison Keillor and Brian McLaren)

Character issues

Christianity: you decide!

Churches: who/what's killing most of them
   in western countries
Claypool, John ('best writing-preacher in the
   English language')
Counselling
Courage
Creation/climate change
Crime
Culture (music, etc)

Death/dying
Diversity
Dreams
Denominations, (Christian: 50,000 of them???)

Economics
Education
Emotions (like fear/guilt/shame/joy)
Enneagram (know who you are)
Environment (enjoying/preserving nature)
Ethics
Eva Burrows (one of several 'best-put-together' women)
Evangelicals
   (why does President Trump like them,
   and sometimes vice-versa)
Evil

Faith/doubt
Families

Fathers
Forgiving others (and yourself!)
Fundamentalisms
Future

Gandhi
God (what is God really like?)
Good & evil

Happiness
Health (including diet, exercise, sleep, etc.)
Healthy churches (popular summary
of two of my post-graduate degrees)
Heroes (female & male, sacred & secular)
Holy Spirit
Hope
Humour

Institutions
International issues
Internet
Islam

Leadership
Love and justice (again)

Manhood
Marriage
Meditation (including 'mindfulness')

Men
Mental health & suicide issues
Ministry as empowerment (my take on why clergy are being sucked in by clericalism)
Miracles: really?
Miscellaneous wisdom: bits & pieces
Mission (why it's good to be useful as well as decorative)
Money, money, money
Morality
Mothers

Niebuhr (both Reinhold and Richard: two more of my heroes)

Old age (I turned 80 in 2017: so I'm a bit of an expert here)
Others/community
Outsiders/marginalised

Parables
Persecution
Politics
Poverty
Prayer (and solitude)
Pride and power

Questions (including the benefits of changing your mind occasionally)

Racism
Refugees

Relationships

Religions (are all religions equally helpful in helping us deal with ultimate issues?)

Rohr, Richard (the Catholic who's probably most heard/read around the world these days

Science

Secular heroes (Mandela and others)

Self-esteem

Sex and romance

Simplicity (the other side of complexity is best)

Sin (especially the 'unpardonable' varieties)

Spirituality

Stott, John (20th century's 'Mr Evangelical', whom I was privileged to know a little)

Stress and burnout

Suffering

Technology/technologies

Time

Trouble

War

Wisdom

Women

Work

Youth

www.ingramcontent.com/pod-product-compliance
Lightning Source LLC
Chambersburg PA
CBHW051951290426
44110CB00015B/2196